SECOND EDITION

VOLUME TWO
Clyde Robert Bulla to Kate DiCamillo

Favorite Children's
AUTHORS *and*
ILLUSTRATORS

E. Russell Primm III, Editor in Chief

ॐ

PO Box 326, Chanhassen, MN 55317-0326
800/599-READ
http://www.childsworld.com

A Note to Our Readers:

The publication dates listed in each author's or illustrator's selected bibliography represent the date of first publication in the United States.

The editors have listed literary awards that were announced prior to August 2006.

Every effort has been made to contact copyright holders of material included in this reference work. If any errors or omissions have occurred, corrections will be made in future editions.

Photographs: 12, 52—Simon & Schuster; 16, 124—Library of Congress; 24, 100, 152—Candlewick Press; 28, 64, 120—Houghton Mifflin; 36—Henry Holt; 40—Das Anndas / Farrar, Straus, and Giroux; 44, 144—Penguin Putnam; 48, 84—Scholastic; 56—Alan McEwen / HarperCollins; 60—George Flowers / HarperCollins; 68—Tobias Cole / Farrar, Straus, and Giroux; 72, 136—Jungsoo Kim / Scholastic; 76—Miramax Books; 80—Bryan Collier; 88—Weston Woods / de Grummond Collection, University of Southern Mississippi; 92, 108—HarperCollins; 104—Pleasant Company; 112—Nina Crews / HarperCollins; 128—Gill Evans / Scholastic; 148—Harcourt.

An Editorial Directions book

Library of Congress Cataloging-in-Publication Data

Favorite children's authors and illustrators / E. Russell Primm III, editor-in-chief. — 2nd ed.
   v. cm.
  Includes bibliographical references and index.
  Contents: v. 1. Verna Aardema to Ashley Bryan.
  ISBN-13: 978-1-59187-057-9 (v.1 : alk. paper)
  ISBN-10: 1-59187-057-7 (v. 1 : alk. paper)
  ISBN-13: 978-1-59187-058-6 (v. 2 : alk. paper)
  ISBN-10: 1-59187-058-5 (v. 2 : alk. paper)
  ISBN-13: 978-1-59187-059-3 (v. 3 : alk. paper)
  ISBN-10: 1-59187-059-3 (v. 3 : alk. paper)
  ISBN-13: 978-1-59187-060-9 (v. 4 : alk. paper)
  ISBN-10: 1-59187-060-7 (v. 4 : alk. paper)
  ISBN-13: 978-1-59187-061-6 (v. 5 : alk. paper)
  ISBN-10: 1-59187-061-5 (v. 5 : alk. paper)
  ISBN-13: 978-1-59187-062-3 (v. 6 : alk. paper)
  ISBN-10: 1-59187-062-3 (v. 6 : alk. paper)
  ISBN-13: 978-1-59187-063-0 (v. 7 : alk. paper)
  ISBN-10: 1-59187-063-1 (v. 7 : alk. paper)
  ISBN-13: 978-1-59187-064-7 (v. 8 : alk. paper)
  ISBN-10: 1-59187-064-X (v. 8 : alk. paper)
  1. Children's literature—Bio-bibliography—Dictionaries—Juvenile literature. 2. Young adult literature Bio-bibliography—Dictionaries—Juvenile literature. 3. Illustrators—Biography—Dictionaries—Juvenile literature. 4. Children—Books and reading—Dictionaries—Juvenile literature. 5. Young Adults—Books and reading—Dictionaries—Juvenile literature. I. Primm, E. Russell, 1958–
  PN1009.A1F38 2007
  809'.8928203—dc22
  [B]   2006011358

First printing.

ABLE OF CONTENTS

6   *Major Children's Author and Illustrator*
      Literary Awards

8   Clyde Robert Bulla

12   Eve Bunting

16   Frances Hodgson Burnett

20   Sheila Burnford

24   John Burningham

28   Virginia Lee Burton

32   Oliver Butterworth

36   Betsy Byars

40   Ann Cameron

44   Eric Carle

48   Peter Catalanotto

52   John Christopher

56   Beverly Cleary

60   Vera Cleaver and Bill Cleaver

64   Andrew Clements

68   Brock Cole

72   Joanna Cole

76   Eoin Colfer

80   Bryan Collier

84   James Lincoln Collier and Christopher Collier

88   Barbara Cooney

92   Floyd Cooper

96   Susan Cooper

100   Lucy Cousins

104   Helen Craig

108   Sharon Creech

112   Donald Crews

116   Christopher Paul Curtis

120   Karen Cushman

124   Roald Dahl

128   Paula Danziger

132   Ingri d'Aulaire and Edgar Parin d'Aulaire

136   Bruce Degen

140   Demi

144   Tomie de Paola

148   David Diaz

152   Kate DiCamillo

156   *Index*

MAJOR CHILDREN'S AUTHOR
AND ILLUSTRATOR LITERARY AWARDS

THE AMERICAN BOOK AWARDS

Awarded from 1980 to 1983 in place of the National Book Award to give national recognition to achievement in several categories of children's literature

THE BOSTON GLOBE–HORN BOOK AWARDS

Established in 1967 by Horn Book *magazine and the* Boston Globe *newspaper to honor the year's best fiction, poetry, nonfiction, and picture books for children*

THE CALDECOTT MEDAL

Established in 1938 and presented by the Association for Library Service to Children division of the American Library Association to illustrators for the most distinguished picture book for children from the preceding year

THE CARNEGIE MEDAL

Established in 1936 and presented by the British Library Association for an outstanding book for children written in English

THE CARTER G. WOODSON BOOK AWARDS

Established in 1974 and presented by the National Council for the Social Studies for the most distinguished social science books appropriate for young readers that depict ethnicity in the United States

THE CORETTA SCOTT KING AWARDS

Established in 1970 in connection with the American Library Association to honor African American authors and illustrators whose books are deemed outstanding, educational, and inspirational

THE HANS CHRISTIAN ANDERSEN MEDAL

Established in 1956 by the International Board on Books for Young People to honor an author or illustrator, living at the time of nomination, whose complete works have made a lasting contribution to children's literature

THE KATE GREENAWAY MEDAL
Established by the Youth Libraries Group of the British Library Association in 1956 to honor illustrators of children's books published in the United Kingdom

THE LAURA INGALLS WILDER AWARD
Established by the Association for Library Service to Children division of the American Library Association in 1954 to honor an author or illustrator whose books, published in the United States, have made a substantial and lasting contribution to children's literature

THE MICHAEL L. PRINTZ AWARD
Established by the Young Adult Library Services division of the American Library Association in 2000 to honor literary excellence in young adult literature (fiction, nonfiction, poetry, or anthology)

THE NATIONAL BOOK AWARDS
Established in 1950 to give national recognition to achievement in fiction, nonfiction, poetry, and young people's literature

THE NEWBERY MEDAL
Established in 1922 and presented by the Association for Library Service to Children division of the American Library Association for the most distinguished contribution to children's literature in the preceding year

THE ORBIS PICTUS AWARD FOR OUTSTANDING NONFICTION
Established in 1990 by the National Council of Teachers of English to honor an outstanding informational book published in the preceding year

THE PURA BELPRÉ AWARD
Established in 1996 and cosponsored by the Association for Library Service to Children division of the American Library Association and the National Association to Promote Library Services to the Spanish Speaking to recognize a writer and illustrator of Latino or Latina background whose works affirm and celebrate the Latino experience

THE SCOTT O'DELL AWARD
Established in 1982 and presented by the O'Dell Award Committee to an American author who writes an outstanding tale of historical fiction for children or young adults that takes place in the New World

Clyde Robert Bulla

Born: January 9, 1914

Clyde Robert Bulla knew from childhood that he wanted to be a writer, but he didn't get much encouragement. Born on a farm near King City, Missouri, on January 9, 1914, he attended a one-room schoolhouse. In class, Clyde began writing stories, verses, and plays. Much of what he learned about writing, he had to teach himself.

As he got older, Clyde Bulla tried to sell his stories to magazines. Editor after editor sent him rejection slips. When he was twenty, he finally sold a story. Then he sold another—and another. The money he earned from his stories helped his family survive the Great Depression.

Finally, Bulla wrote a novel that was published with little success. He wrote two

BULLA HAS WRITTEN THE STORY OF HIS OWN LIFE. *A GRAIN OF WHEAT: A WRITER BEGINS* TELLS OF HIS DETERMINATION TO BE A STORYTELLER AND WRITER, EVEN THOUGH HIS FAMILY DID NOT ENCOURAGE HIM.

more books, but no one wanted to publish them. Bulla knew he wanted to put words together, but he didn't know what he wanted to write.

As a young man, Bulla went to work for the newspaper in King City. He set type, kept the accounts, collected bills, and wrote a weekly column.

One day, Emma Celeste Thibodaux, a teacher friend, suggested he write for children. "I have no ideas," he told her. She gave him one. Bulla didn't want to disappoint her, so he wrote a story using her idea. It was called *The Donkey Cart.* He sent it to an agent, who did not think it would sell.

Then Thibodaux met a children's author named Lois Lenski.

A Selected Bibliography of Bulla's Work

A Tree Is a Plant (2001)
The Paint Brush Kid (1999)
The Story of Valentine's Day (1999)
A Place for Angels (1996)
The Christmas Coat (1989)
Singing Sam (1989)
The Chalk Box Kid (1987)
A Grain of Wheat: A Writer Begins (1985)
The Cardboard Crown (1984)
Charlie's House (1983)
Dandelion Hill (1982)
Almost a Hero (1981)
A Lion to Guard Us (1981)
Conquista! (1978)
The Beast of Lor (1977)
Shoeshine Girl (1975)
Pocahontas and the Strangers (1971)
Benito (1961)
Squanto, Friend of the White Men (1954)
Riding the Pony Express (1948)
The Donkey Cart (1946)

Thibodaux sent Lenski some of Bulla's newspaper columns and told her he had written a children's book. When Lenski asked to see it, Bulla sent her the manuscript for *The Donkey Cart*. Within a week, a New York publisher accepted the manuscript!

> "[Riding the Pony Express] *fell short of my hopes and expectations. I began to learn that no book would ever be the wonderful work that I had planned. But I had found the kind of writing that I wanted to do—the kind I was meant to do.*"

The publisher asked Bulla to rewrite the book and take out some of the chapters. *The Donkey Cart* was published in 1946, with illustrations by Lois Lenski. Bulla wasn't pleased with the book. It wasn't as good as he had hoped it would be. But the editor asked for another book.

Bulla then wrote about the Pony Express. He thought the story of the men who had carried the mail on horseback would be exciting for children. But when *Riding the Pony Express* was published, he was disappointed again and realized that no book would ever be perfect.

One of his best-known works is *The Chalk Box Kid*. It is about a boy who doesn't feel he fits in at a new school. He discovers a burned-out building and a box of chalk, and he draws a garden on the building. Bulla has said that he often felt uncomfortable in new surroundings, like the boy in the book. "I gave Gregory something I've always wished for: a

WHEN YOUNG CLYDE TOLD HIS FATHER HE WANTED TO BE A WRITER, HIS FATHER DISCOURAGED HIM. "YOU CAN'T BE A WRITER," HE SAID. "YOU HAVEN'T BEEN ANYWHERE OR DONE ANYTHING. YOU DON'T HAVE ANYTHING TO WRITE ABOUT."

big, blank wall that I could cover with my own drawings," he said.

Clyde Robert Bulla is a talented amateur painter as well as a musician. He has composed songs for his books. He has also set some of Lois Lenski's poems to music.

Bulla lived in California for fifty years.

Then he returned to Missouri, where he continues to write.

> *"As soon as I discovered words and what they meant and what they could be made to mean, my path was set. I was going to be a writer."*

WHERE TO FIND OUT MORE ABOUT CLYDE ROBERT BULLA

BOOKS

Bulla, Clyde Robert. *A Grain of Wheat: A Writer Begins.* Boston: David R. Godine, 1985.

Rockman, Connie, ed. *Eighth Book of Junior Authors and Illustrators.* New York: H. W. Wilson Company, 2000.

St. James Guide to Children's Writers. Detroit: St. James Press, 1999.

WEB SITES

CLYDE ROBERT BULLA HOME PAGE
http://mowrites4kids.drury.edu/authors/bulla/
For a biographical sketch of Clyde Robert Bulla, plus an address for fan mail, and a booklist

EDUCATIONAL PAPERBACK ASSOCIATION
http://edupaperback.org/showauth.cfm?authid=237
To read an autobiographical sketch and a booklist for Clyde Robert Bulla

-----

BULLA REMEMBERS THAT SOME OF HIS CLASSMATES IN THE ONE-ROOM SCHOOLHOUSE HAD A HARD TIME READING. KEEPING THEM IN MIND, HE TRIES TO MAKE HIS BOOKS EASY TO READ—AND INTERESTING ENOUGH TO HOLD A CHILD'S ATTENTION.

Eve Bunting

Born: December 19, 1928

Although she was not sure she would ever be a writer, Eve Bunting always had a gift for storytelling. It was an important part of her life even as a child. Bunting has used this gift to become the author of such favorite children's books as *Smoky Night, One More Flight,* and *Ghost of Summer.*

She was born Anne Evelyn Bolton in Maghera, Northern Ireland, on December 19, 1928. Her father read stories and poetry to her every day. Eve also wrote her own stories and read them to her father. Then they talked about the stories and the words she chose for her writing. Her father helped her understand how to improve her stories.

BUNTING HAS PUBLISHED SEVERAL BOOKS UNDER THE NAME EVELYN BOLTON.

Growing up in Northern Ireland was difficult for Eve. A great deal of conflict existed between Catholics and Protestants there. The Bolton family was Protestant. Eve saw how the Protestant people discriminated against the Catholics. This prejudice was difficult for her to accept. It was something she never forgot.

Eve Bolton graduated from Northern Ireland's Methodist College in 1945. She went on to study at Queen's University in Belfast. There she met Edward Davison Bunting. She dropped out of college and married him in 1951. Because they wanted to get away from the political tensions in Northern Ireland, Eve Bunting and her husband

By Eve Bunting · Illustrated by Ronald Himler

A Selected Bibliography of Bunting's Work

One Green Apple (2006)
My Red Balloon (2005)
I Love You, Too! (2004)
Anna's Table (2003)
The Bones of Fred McFee (2002)
The Days of Summer (2001)
The Summer of Riley (2001)
Dear Wish Fairy (2000)
Doll Baby (2000)
Butterfly House (1999)
Can You Do This, Old Badger? (1999)
The Blue and the Gray (1996)
Smoky Night (1994)
Fly Away Home (1991)
The Wall (1990)
The Ghost Children (1989)
The Wednesday Surprise (1989)
How Many Days to America?: A Thanksgiving Story (1988)
Sixth-Grade Sleepover (1986)
Face at the Edge of the World (1985)
Karen Kepplewhite Is the World's Best Kisser (1983)
The Big Red Barn (1979)
Ghost of Summer (1977)
One More Flight (1976)
The Two Giants (1972)

> *"I like to write for every child. For every age, for every interest. That is why I have such a variety of works from preschool, through the middle grades, and beyond."*

moved their three children to San Francisco, California.

Her husband was busy with his career so Bunting stayed at home to take care of their children. Several years after arriving in California, she decided to take a writing class at a local community college. She rediscovered her love for storytelling and began writing for children.

Bunting's first book, *The Two Giants,* was published in 1972. She was more than forty years old when it was published. Since that time, Bunting has written more than 150 fiction and nonfiction books. She has also written many articles for children's magazines.

Many of her books deal with difficult problems. The subjects of her books include homelessness, poverty, racial prejudice, death, war, and violence. "I may have had books turned down because they're not good, but I've never had one turned down because it was saying something people might consider not suitable for

> *"I have succeeded beyond my wildest dreams. My success has been a constant surprise. I often think, 'How can all these things happen to this little kid from Maghera?'"*

EVE BUNTING COLLABORATED WITH ARTIST DAVID DIAZ ON *SMOKY NIGHT*. SHE WROTE THE TEXT, AND HE DID THE ILLUSTRATIONS. (THE ARTWORK ENDED UP EARNING THE BOOK THE 1995 CALDECOTT MEDAL.)

children," Bunting notes. She also writes books on less serious topics—books that are fun and full of joy. She has even written nonfiction books about whales and sharks for SeaWorld.

Today, Eve Bunting lives in Pasadena, California, with her husband. She has four grandchildren. She continues to write books and magazine articles for children.

❧

WHERE TO FIND OUT MORE ABOUT EVE BUNTING

BOOKS

McElmeel, Sharron L. *100 Most Popular Children's Authors: Biographical Sketches and Bibliographies*. Englewood, Colo.: Libraries Unlimited, 1999.

McElmeel, Sharron L. *100 Most Popular Picture Book Authors and Illustrators: Biographical Sketches and Bibliographies*. Englewood, Colo.: Libraries Unlimited, 2000.

McGinty, Alice B. *Meet Eve Bunting*. New York: PowerKids Press, 2002.

Silvey, Anita, ed. *The Essential Guide to Children's Books and Their Creators*. Boston: Houghton Mifflin Company, 2002.

WEB SITES

EDUCATIONAL PAPERBACK ASSOCIATION
http://edupaperback.org/showauth.cfm?authid=18
To read an autobiographical account and booklist for Eve Bunting

KIDSREADS.COM
http://www.kidsreads.com/authors/au-bunting-eve.asp
To read a biographical account of Eve Bunting and a description of *The Summer of Riley*

————

BUNTING HAS RECEIVED MANY AWARDS AND HONORS FOR HER BOOKS, INCLUDING THE GOLDEN KITE AWARD FROM THE SOCIETY OF CHILDREN'S BOOK WRITERS AND ILLUSTRATORS IN 1976 FOR *ONE MORE FLIGHT*.

Frances Hodgson Burnett

Born: November 24, 1849
Died: October 29, 1924

Many children today have read the popular books *The Secret Garden* and *A Little Princess.* It is hard to believe that the author, Frances Hodgson Burnett, was born more than 150 years ago!

On November 24, 1849, Frances Eliza Hodgson was born in Manchester, England. She was one of five children, and her father owned a furniture store. When Frances was four years old, her father died. Her mother worked hard to raise the five children and keep the store running. In the 1860s, business in England was not good. It was hard to make money.

Finally, in 1865, Frances's mother had to sell the store. She packed up her family and moved

THE AMERICAN BOY IN *LITTLE LORD FAUNTLEROY* HAS
LONG CURLS AND WEARS A VELVET SUIT WITH A LACE COLLAR.
THESE CLOTHES WERE POPULAR FOR BOYS AT THE TIME.

them to the United States to join her brother. Frances and her family settled near Knoxville, Tennessee. Although life in Tennessee was not much easier than it had been in England, Frances liked it there.

By now, Frances Hodgson was a teenager who enjoyed writing. She had written many stories for fun. She decided to try selling a story to a magazine. She was successful on her first try! During the next few years, she had stories published in many American magazines. Over the next ten years, Hodgson married Dr. Swan Burnett and continued writing. She first wrote short stories and novels for adults, then tried writing for children.

"All she thought about the key was that if it was the key to the closed garden, and she could find out where the door was, she could perhaps open it and see what was inside the walls, and what had happened to the old rose-trees."
—*from* **The Secret Garden**

In 1886, Frances Hodgson Burnett published her children's novel *Little Lord Fauntleroy*. It was a hit immediately. In fact, Burnett was asked to turn it into a play. It became one of the best-selling works of the time! Because of her success, Burnett became famous. She was well known for her many travels and her colorful, interesting clothing.

Sadly, her personal life was not as successful as her writing career. Her marriage was not a happy one. She had two sons, Lionel

LITTLE LORD FAUNTLEROY WAS MADE INTO A MOVIE FIVE TIMES: IN 1914, 1922, 1936, 1980, AND 1995!

By FRANCES HODGSON BURNETT
Illustrated by TASHA TUDOR

A Selected Bibliography of Burnett's Work

The Lost Prince (1915)
The Secret Garden (1911)
Racketty-Packetty House (1906)
A Little Princess (1905)
Little Lord Fauntleroy (1886)

and Vivian. At age seventeen, Lionel became ill with tuberculosis. For several years after he died, Burnett's stories were sad and gloomy.

Burnett kept writing plays and stories for adults. She also continued to write novels for children. In 1905, Burnett published the children's book *A Little Princess.* This was a newer version of a book she had written earlier called *Sara Crewe: Or, What Happened at Miss Minchin's.* It is one of Burnett's most popular stories.

In 1911, Burnett wrote *The Secret Garden.* It, too, was popular immediately.

One of Burnett's last books was *The Lost Prince.* That book did not become as popular as her other famous children's books. Burnett lived on Long Island in New York, where she wrote, entertained friends, and gardened until she died in 1924.

> " 'A bit of earth,' he said to himself, and Mary thought that somehow she must have reminded him of something. When he stopped and spoke to her his dark eyes looked almost soft and kind."
> —from **The Secret Garden**

WHERE TO FIND OUT MORE ABOUT FRANCES HODGSON BURNETT

BOOKS

Bixler, Phyllis. *The Secret Garden: Nature's Magic.* New York: Twayne Publishers, 1996.

Carpenter, Angelica Shirley, and Jean Shirley. *Frances Hodgson Burnett: Beyond the Secret Garden.* Minneapolis: Lerner, 1990.

Greene, Carol. *Frances Hodgson Burnett: Author of the Secret Garden.* Chicago: Childrens Press, 1995.

WEB SITES

THE LITERATURE NETWORK
http://www.online-literature.com/burnett/
To read a brief biographical sketch and booklist for Frances Hodgson Burnett

WOMEN IN AMERICAN HISTORY FROM BRITANNICA
http://www.britannica.com/women/articles/Burnett_Frances_Eliza_Hodgson.html
To read a biographical sketch of Frances Hodgson Burnett

BURNETT LOVED TO WRITE AS A CHILD AND WROTE ABOUT THAT IN HER BOOK *THE ONE I KNEW THE BEST OF ALL: A MEMORY IN THE MIND OF A CHILD.*

Sheila Burnford

Born: May 11, 1918
Died: April 20, 1984

Sheila Burnford was a versatile author. She wrote fiction and nonfiction for children and adults. She is best known, however, for her very first novel, *The Incredible Journey*. This tale of three lost pets and their journey home has become a classic.

Burnford was born Sheila Philip Cochrane Every in Scotland in 1918. Sheila was educated at St. George's School, a private girls' school in Edinburgh, Scotland. Then she attended Harrogate College in Yorkshire, England.

World War II (1939–1945) had an impact on the young woman's life. From 1939 to 1941, she volunteered in the Royal Naval hospitals. Then she served as a volunteer ambulance driver until 1942. While volunteering, she met Dr. David Burnford, a surgeon in the British Royal Navy. They married in 1941. The couple had three daughters—Peronelle Philip, Elizabeth Jonquil, and Juliet Sheila.

THE 1963 MOVIE *THE INCREDIBLE JOURNEY* WAS REMADE IN 1993 AS *HOMEWARD BOUND*. A SEQUEL, *HOMEWARD BOUND II*, CAME OUT IN 1996.

As the war dragged on, Burnford spent many nights at home alone in the dark. The British government often ordered all lights off so as not to attract enemy bombs, and Burnford's husband was away on duty. To pass the time, she read to her bull terrier, Bill.

In 1948, the family moved to Canada, settling in Port Arthur, Ontario. Throughout the 1950s, Burnford wrote articles about Canada for British magazines, as well as writing scripts for local puppet shows at the Port Arthur Puppetry Club. As time passed, the family acquired two more pets—a Labrador retriever and a Siamese cat. Burnford was fascinated by the way the pets communicated with one another

A Selected Bibliography of Burnford's Work

Bel Ria: Dog of War (1977)
Mr. Noah and the Second Flood (1973)
One Woman's Arctic (1972)
Without Reserve (1969)
The Fields of Noon (1964)
The Incredible Journey (1961)

> "Animals remain unchanged, in character, by the winds of politics, greed, terrorism, oil spillage and all the daily horror with which the media bombard our minds."

and even seemed to follow each other's directions.

After Bill, the bull terrier, died, Burnford began writing *The Incredible Journey*. Set in the wilderness of northern Ontario, it tells of the remarkable adventures of three family pets. Burnford's choice of characters was easy—a bull terrier, a Labrador retriever, and a Siamese cat. The three face dangers and hardships as they cross the wilderness to find their way home. Although the animals don't talk, Burnford describes their thoughts and feelings vividly. Published in 1961, the book was an immediate best seller. Walt Disney Studios made it into a movie in 1963.

Burnford covered many subjects in her later books. She spent two summers on Baffin Island in Canada's Arctic region. There she lived among the Inuit people, taking part in their traditional activities and observing the environment. She wrote about her experiences in an adult nonfiction book, *One Woman's Arctic*. Her children's fable *Mr. Noah and the Second Flood* warns about the dangers of pollution. Burnford's final book was another animal story—*Bel Ria: Dog of War*. It's the true story

---

BURNFORD DEDICATED *THE INCREDIBLE JOURNEY* TO HER THREE CHILDREN.

of a tough little terrier
that touches many lives
during World War II.

In her later years,
Burnford moved back
to England. She lived in Bucklers Hard, a small village in Hampshire,
on England's southern coast. There she died of cancer at the age of
sixty-five.

> *"I'm a back-to-the-wall, deadline-looming, undisciplined-in-time writer whose mind starts functioning toward evening."*

≈

WHERE TO FIND OUT MORE ABOUT SHEILA BURNFORD

BOOKS

Berger, Laura Standley, ed. *Twentieth-Century Children's Writers*. 4th ed. Detroit: St. James Press, 1995.

Rockman, Connie C., ed. *Eighth Book of Junior Authors and Illustrators*. New York: H. W. Wilson, 2000.

Silvey, Anita, ed. *The Essential Guide to Children's Books and Their Creators*. Boston: Houghton Mifflin Company, 2002.

WEB SITES

ENCYCLOPAEDIA BRITANNICA
http://www.britannica.com/ebi/article-9318296
For a biography and description of her books

TEACHING RESOURCES
http://www.loveyourdog.com/resources.html#journey
For a guide to teaching both the book *The Incredible Journey* and the movie made from it, *Homeward Bound*

BURNFORD'S HOBBIES INCLUDED STUDYING ASTRONOMY AND MUSHROOMS.

John Burningham

Born: April 27, 1936

John Burningham was born in Farnham, Surrey, in England, on April 27, 1936. When he was a boy, his parents sent him to ten different private schools before settling on Summerhill, a famous experimental school. One of Summerhill's rules is that children don't have to attend class if they don't want to, so John Burningham spent much of his time working in the art room. "The best preparation for my work now was the fact that I wasn't pressured as a child," he says. "Mucking about is essential for everybody."

When he was seventeen, John Burningham became a conscientious objector. A conscientious objector is someone who will not join an army or take part in a war. At that time, Britain expected all young people to serve in the

---

MR. GUMPY AND SHIRLEY HAVE EACH APPEARED IN TWO OF HIS BOOKS, BUT BURNINGHAM IS NOT LIKELY TO WRITE MORE ABOUT THESE CHARACTERS. "[U]NLESS I CAN FEEL THAT I AM BREAKING NEW TERRITORY, I DON'T WANT TO CREATE," HE SAYS.

armed forces. As an alternative, Burningham had to do public service work. He worked with an ambulance unit, and he helped clear slums and build schools. Some of his work was done in other countries, including Israel, where he returned later to work on a film.

When Burningham came back to England, he ran into a friend who was attending the Central School of Art there. Art school sounded like a good idea to Burningham, so he applied and got in.

After art school, Burningham worked as a teacher and designed posters for London Transport. He wanted to work as an illustrator, but the publishers he talked to said he needed more

Mr. Gumpy's Outing
John Burningham

A Selected Bibliography of Burningham's Work

When We Were Young (2005)
Colors (2003)
Hushabye (2000)
Whaddayamean (1999)
Cloudland (1996)
Courtney (1994)
First Steps: Letters, Numbers, Colors, Opposites (1994)
Harvey Slumfenburger's Christmas Present (1993)
Aldo (1991)
Hey! Get off Our Train (1989)
Where's Julius? (1986)
Cluck Baa (1984)
Granpa (1984)
Avocado Baby (1982)
Time to Get out of the Bath, Shirley (1978)
Come Away from the Water, Shirley (1977)
The School (1974)
The Snow (1974)
Mr. Gumpy's Outing (1970)
Borka: The Adventures of a Goose with No Feathers (1963)

Burningham's Major Literary Awards

1972 Boston Globe–Horn Book Picture Book Award
1970 Kate Greenaway Medal
  Mr. Gumpy's Outing

1963 Kate Greenaway Medal
  Borka: The Adventures of a Goose with No Feathers

experience. In frustration, he wrote a book of his own and illustrated it. It was an "ugly duckling" story about an unusual goose. When the book, *Borka: The Adventures of a Goose with No Feathers,* was published in 1963, it won the Kate Greenaway Medal. Burningham hadn't really intended to go into children's books, but his first effort was so successful that he stuck with it.

> *"I enjoy making children's books—and I use the word 'making' rather than 'writing' because I think of my books as a series of drawings held together by a thread of text. I enjoy it because it allows me to work with the maximum freedom and to carry out my own ideas."*

In 1970, after writing and illustrating several animal stories, Burningham published *Mr. Gumpy's Outing,* another prizewinner and one of his best-loved books. In the story, Mr. Gumpy goes for a ride in his boat. Two children, a rabbit, a dog, a cat, and a sheep join him. All of them promise to behave, but things go wrong and everyone ends up in the water.

Many of Burningham's books are about children who go off into a world of fantasy. There's Shirley in *Come Away from the Water, Shirley* and *Time to Get out of the Bath, Shirley.* Shirley ignores her parents' warning to stay safe—but only in her imagination. In *Aldo,* a lonely girl has an imaginary rabbit for a friend. *Where's Julius?* is the story of a boy who can't come to dinner because he's too busy with fantastic adventures.

BURNINGHAM LIKES TO WORK ON SEVERAL PROJECTS AT THE SAME TIME. HE COMPARES IT TO BEING AN ACTOR IN A REPERTORY THEATER, WHERE YOU PERFORM IN ONE PLAY WHILE YOU'RE REHEARSING FOR THE NEXT ONE.

Some of Burningham's most recent books have taken a more serious turn. *Hey! Get off Our Train* is about endangered species, while *Whaddayamean* is a conversation between two children and God about war, the environment, and global warming.

Burningham is married to another award-winning writer and illustrator of children's books—Helen Oxenbury. They have a son and two daughters. Burningham lives with his family in London.

> *"People often say what terrible nagging parents I portray, but really they're not terrible—children are annoying. You have to realize that children are just people. The difference is that they have less experience."*

❧

WHERE TO FIND OUT MORE ABOUT JOHN BURNINGHAM

BOOKS

McElmeel, Sharron L. *100 Most Popular Picture Book Authors and Illustrators: Biographical Sketches and Bibliographies.* Englewood, Colo.: Libraries Unlimited, 2000.

Silvey, Anita, ed. *The Essential Guide to Children's Books and Their Creators.* Boston: Houghton Mifflin Company, 2002.

WEB SITE
MAGIC PENCIL
http://magicpencil.britishcouncil.org/artists/burningham/
To read a biographical sketch and booklist

―――

THOUGH HE'S A SUCCESSFUL ILLUSTRATOR, BURNINGHAM STILL FINDS IT HARD TO TURN OUT GOOD PICTURES. HE SAYS HE OFTEN GETS TO THE POINT WHERE HE FEELS AS IF HE HAS NO ABILITIES AT ALL. "THIS CAN BE QUITE DEPRESSING," HE EXPLAINS.

Virginia Lee Burton

Born: August 30, 1909
Died: October 15, 1968

Artist and author Virginia Lee Burton wrote only seven children's books. Several of her books are considered classics, though. *The Little House* is generally considered her best work. Burton imagined a house that was happy when it was in the country and sad when the city was built up around it. The great-granddaughter of the man who built it rescues the sad house and moves it back to the country, where it is once again lived in and happy. Burton's books often give human characteristics to inanimate objects.

Virginia Lee Burton was born on August 30, 1909, in Newton Centre, Massachusetts. Her family moved to Sonora, California, when she was seven. After high school, Virginia won a scholarship to study

---

IN 1967, VIRGINIA LEE BURTON GAVE THE SAN FRANCISCO PUBLIC LIBRARY THE ORIGINAL ILLUSTRATIONS FROM *MAYBELLE, THE CABLE CAR.*

ballet and art at the California School of Fine Arts in San Francisco. Later she studied art at the Boston Museum of Fine Arts School.

After school, Burton worked for the *Boston Transcript* newspaper, drawing sketches for the music, dance, and theater sections. After performances, Burton sometimes stayed up all night, sketching the actors and dancers from memory.

In 1931, she married George Demetrios, a sculptor who had been her teacher at the Boston Museum of Fine Arts School. They had two sons. The family lived in Folly Cove near Gloucester, Massachusetts.

Burton began writing books to please her children. She tried to choose subjects she thought would interest them. Her first book was about a dust particle. Thirteen publishers rejected it, and it was never published. She abandoned the story when her three-year-old son fell asleep while she was reading it to him!

> *"I literally draw my books first and write down the text after. . . . I pin the sketched pages in sequence on the walls of my studio so I can see the books as a whole."*

Her first published book was *Choo Choo: The Story of a Little Engine Who Ran Away.* After that she wrote several books in which machines have human feelings and the ability to move about as they

---

THE HAGGERTY MUSEUM AT MARQUETTE UNIVERSITY IN WISCONSIN HAD A SPECIAL EXHIBIT OF BURTON'S WORK IN 2002. THE EXHIBITION CELEBRATED THE PUBLICATION OF A BOOK CALLED *VIRGINIA LEE BURTON: A LIFE IN ART.*

A Selected Bibliography of Burton's Work

Life Story (1962)

Maybelle, the Cable Car (1952)

The Emperor's New Clothes (Illustrations only, 1949)

Song of Robin Hood (Illustrations only, 1947)

Katy and the Big Snow (1943)

The Little House (1942)

Calico, the Wonder Horse; or, The Saga of Stewy Stinker (1941)

Mike Mulligan and His Steam Shovel (1939)

Choo Choo: The Story of a Little Engine Who Ran Away (1937)

Sad-Faced Boy (Illustrations only, 1937)

Burton's Major Literary Awards

1948 Caldecott Honor Book
  Song of Robin Hood

1943 Caldecott Medal
  The Little House

please. Her second book was *Mike Mulligan and His Steam Shovel,* a tale about a steam shovel that is left behind when better equipment is invented. Burton wrote *Calico, the Wonder Horse; or, The Saga of Stewy Stinker* to keep her sons from reading comic books. She designed the book to resemble a comic book with subject matter that she felt was more appropriate for children their age.

Burton worked in pen and ink and on scratchboard. When making a work on scratchboard, the artist uses a knife to scratch the drawing on a surface coated with black ink. The scratches reveal the white paper underneath, so that a scratchboard work looks like a negative of a

pen-and-ink drawing. This technique is
not often used today.

Writing the text of her books was
more difficult for Burton than creating
the pictures. She did both illustrations
and text though, because she wanted to

> *"One must never 'write down' to children. They sense adult condescension in an instant, and they turn away from it."*

have complete control over her books. Her writing style was plain and
straightforward. She chose each word of her stories carefully.

Virginia Lee Burton's interest in children's books faded as her
children grew older. She died in 1968 in Boston.

❧

WHERE TO FIND OUT MORE ABOUT VIRGINIA LEE BURTON

BOOKS

Hedblad, Alan. *Something about the Author.* Vol. 100. Detroit: Gale Research, 1999.

McElmeel, Sharron L. *100 Most Popular Picture Book Authors and Illustrators: Biographical Sketches and Bibliographies.* Englewood, Colo.: Libraries Unlimited, 2000.

Silvey, Anita, ed. *The Essential Guide to Children's Books and Their Creators.* Boston: Houghton Mifflin Company, 2002.

WEB SITES

HOUGHTON MIFFLIN: VIRGINIA LEE BURTON
http://www.houghtonmifflinbooks.com/features/mike_mulligan/biohome.shtml
To read a biography of Virginia Lee Burton, to learn more about her family, and for
activities related to her books

———

FOR BURTON, THE ILLUSTRATIONS WERE MORE IMPORTANT
THAN THE TEXT OF A BOOK. SOMETIMES HER PICTURES HAVE A CIRCULAR
MOTION TO THEM THAT SEEMS TO REFLECT HER BALLET BACKGROUND.

Oliver Butterworth

Born: May 23, 1915
Died: September 17, 1990

In children's literature, two egg stories that stand out as classics are the old fable *The Goose That Laid the Golden Egg* and a fable for modern times—*The Enormous Egg* by Oliver Butterworth. Both are insightful tales that reveal a lot about human nature.

Oliver Butterworth was born in Hartford, Connecticut, in 1915. He and his two siblings grew up in a farmhouse near Hartford, where they were surrounded by pastures and woods. After the death of their mother, their father raised them on his own.

Oliver spent his high-school years at Kent School in Kent, Connecticut. He attended this boarding school for boys from 1930 to 1933, then enrolled in Dartmouth College in Hanover, New Hampshire. After graduating in 1937, he began teaching English and Latin at his old high school. Butterworth devoted the next fifty years of his life to teaching. He married Miriam Brooks in 1940. They had four children—Michael, Timothy, Dan, and Kate.

THE DINOSAUR IN *THE ENORMOUS EGG* WAS NAMED UNCLE BEAZLEY. A STATUE OF UNCLE BEAZLEY STANDS ON THE GROUNDS OF THE NATIONAL ZOO IN WASHINGTON, D.C.

Butterworth continued his studies. In 1947, he received a master's degree in education from Middlebury College in Vermont. From 1947 to 1949, he taught at the Junior School in West Hartford, Connecticut. Beginning in 1949, he served as an English instructor at Hartford College for Women. He remained at this post until the late 1980s.

In the 1950s, Butterworth was disturbed by the activities of Senator Joseph McCarthy. The Wisconsin senator was trying to root out Communist influences in every corner of American life. Butterworth believed that McCarthy was trampling on Americans' basic freedoms. The only way he felt he could respond was to write. So in

A Selected Bibliography of Butterworth's Work

A Visit to the Big House (1987)
The First Blueberry Pig (1986)
The Narrow Passage (1973)
The Trouble with Jenny's Ear (1960)
The Enormous Egg (1956)

> *"I thought if I could write a book that sounded like a twelve-year-old talking, then children would like it. It seemed to work."*

1956, he wrote *The Enormous Egg*, a fanciful story that includes an evil senator.

Butterworth's family members were the first to hear the story. As he finished writing each section, he read it to them in the evenings. The public loved the story as much as Butterworth's family did. Once it was published, *The Enormous Egg* was wildly popular, and it's still a favorite today.

The Enormous Egg tells about a baby dinosaur that hatches out of a hen's egg. The dino grows so big that people are afraid it will eat the whole state of New Hampshire. Many characters want to use the dinosaur for selfish reasons. One is a senator who tries to have the dino killed. He argues that the dino is useless, out of place, and a drain on taxpayers' money. But the citizens ultimately rally to save the dino. Even today, people hail *The Enormous Egg* as a fable about the triumph of American freedoms.

Butterworth published several more books for children. In *The Trouble with Jenny's Ear*, a girl can hear what others are thinking. In *A Visit to the Big House*, two children go to see their father in prison for the first time.

BUTTERWORTH ADMIRED AUTHOR MARK TWAIN, WHO ONCE LIVED IN
BUTTERWORTH'S HOMETOWN OF HARTFORD.

Butterworth died of cancer in West Hartford at the age of seventy-five. Before he died, he was working on a story called *Orrie's Run*. Although it was never published as a book, the *Hartford Courant* newspaper printed it in 2002.

> *"I see my child characters as 'innocent' persons who find themselves having to make moral or personal decisions on the basis of their own inner feelings or instincts or convictions."*

WHERE TO FIND OUT MORE ABOUT OLIVER BUTTERWORTH

BOOKS

Berger, Laura Standley, ed. *Twentieth-Century Children's Writers.* 4th ed. Detroit: St. James Press, 1995.

Sutherland, Zena. *Children & Books.* 9th ed. New York: Allyn & Bacon, 1997.

WEB SITE

FAMILY FIRST
http://www.familyfirst.net/famlife/childrenclassics.asp
To see a list of books, including *The Enormous Egg,* suitable for children ages eight and up

MAJORITY REPORT
http://www.majorityreportradio.com/weblog/archives/001208.php
To read about Miss Beazley, the White House terrier, and Uncle Beazley from *The Enormous Egg*

THE ENORMOUS EGG HAS BEEN MADE INTO A PLAY, A TV SHOW, AND A MOVIE.

Betsy Byars

Born: August 7, 1928

First, Betsy Byars wanted to work with animals in a zoo. Then she thought she wanted to become a mathematician. Instead, Betsy Byars became a children's author, and she has published more than fifty books for children and young adults. Her most famous books include *The Moon and I, The Summer of the Swans,* and *The Night Swimmers.*

Betsy Cromer was born on August 7, 1928, in Charlotte, North Carolina. Her family lived in the city and then moved to a small village nearby. Her parents read many books and encouraged Betsy to read. She loved to read as a little girl but did not have much interest in writing.

Betsy attended public schools in North Carolina. After she graduated from high school, she went to Furman University for two years. When she started college, her father had wanted her to study

---

BETSY BYARS'S BOOKS HAVE BEEN TRANSLATED INTO NINETEEN DIFFERENT LANGUAGES.

math. She soon learned that she was not interested in math and she decided to study English.

Cromer left Furman University and went back to Charlotte to attend Queens College. She graduated in 1950 with a degree in English. At college, she met Edward Byars. He was teaching engineering at another university nearby. She married him shortly after she graduated from Queens College.

"When I was a girl growing up in the Carolinas, I didn't want to be a writer. I didn't know any writers—I'd never seen one. But their photographs looked funny, as if they'd been taken to a taxidermist and stuffed."

A Selected Bibliography of Byars's Work

Boo's Dinosaur (2006)
Little Horse of His Own (2004)
Little Horse (2001)
My Dog, My Hero (2000)
Death's Door (1997)
Dead Letter (1996)
Bingo Brown, Gypsy Lover (1992)
The Moon and I (1991)
Wanted—Mud Blossom (1991)
Bingo Brown and the Language of Love (1989)
Beans on the Roof (1988)
The Blossoms Meet the Vulture Lady (1986)
Cracker Jackson (1985)
The Two-Thousand-Pound Goldfish (1982)
The Night Swimmers (1980)
The Pinballs (1977)
The TV Kid (1976)
The 18th Emergency (1973)
The Summer of the Swans (1970)
The Midnight Fox (1968)
Clementine (1962)

Byars's Major Literary Awards

1981 National Book Award
1980 Boston Globe–Horn Book Fiction Award
   The Night Swimmers

1971 Newbery Medal
   The Summer of the Swans

Edward Byars enrolled at the University of Illinois as a graduate student. Betsy Byars took care of their children while her husband was studying. She had never considered a career as a writer, but she found that she had many hours to fill.

Betsy Byars began her career writing magazine articles. As her children grew older and learned to read, she began writing stories for them. Her interest in writing soon expanded and she began work on her first children's book. Byars's first book, *Clementine,* was published in 1962. Nine publishing companies rejected this book before it was finally printed.

"I've had moments of great satisfaction, deep disappointment, depression, elation, surprise, rejection, acceptance, fun, sorrow, laughter, tears—you name it, I've had it. I've had every emotion but one. In all those forty years, sitting in a room all by myself, typing, I've never once been bored."

Byars gets most of the ideas for her books from real life. "I write realistic fiction so most of my inspiration comes from things that really happen," Byars notes. "I find many of my ideas for my books in things that happen around me." She gets ideas from reading newspapers and magazines. Other books start with things that happen to her or to people she knows.

BYARS AND HER HUSBAND LIVE NEAR AN AIRSTRIP. THE GROUND FLOOR OF THEIR HOUSE IS A HANGAR WHERE THEY KEEP THEIR PLANE.

Byars lives with her husband in South Carolina. She does most of her writing in winter and spends her summers at their cabin. Byars and her husband are both pilots and enjoy flying gliders and planes. She still writes for young audiences and is always working on a writing project.

❧

WHERE TO FIND OUT MORE ABOUT BETSY BYARS

BOOKS

Cammarano, Rita. *Betsy Byars.* Broomall, Pa.: Chelsea House, 2002.

McElmeel, Sharron L. *100 Most Popular Children's Authors: Biographical Sketches and Bibliographies.* Englewood, Colo.: Libraries Unlimited, 1999.

Moran, Karen A. *A Visit with Betsy Byars.* Fort Atkinson, Wis.: Alleyside Press, 2001.

Rockman, Connie C., ed. *The Ninth Book of Junior Authors and Illustrators.* New York: H. W. Wilson Company, 2004.

Silvey, Anita, ed. *The Essential Guide to Children's Books and Their Creators.* Boston: Houghton Mifflin Company, 2002.

WEB SITES

CAROL HURST'S CHILDREN'S LITERATURE SITE
http://www.carolhurst.com/authors/byars.html
To read a biographical sketch of Betsy Byars

EDUCATIONAL PAPERBACK ASSOCIATION
http://edupaperback.org/showauth.cfm?authid=19
To read an autobiographical sketch and booklist for Betsy Byars

TEACHERS@RANDOM
http://www.randomhouse.com/author/results.pperl?authorid=3960
To read a biographical sketch and fun facts about Betsy Byars

---

BETSY BYARS HAS FOUR ADULT CHILDREN. TWO OF HER DAUGHTERS—BETSY DUFFEY AND LAURIE MYERS—ALSO WRITE BOOKS FOR CHILDREN.

Ann Cameron

Born: October 21, 1943

In the stories Ann Cameron tells, her characters are energetic, engaging, and intelligent—much like Cameron herself. She was inspired to write her first really successful book, *The Stories Julian Tells,* by the tales a South African friend told her about his childhood experiences. Julian and his little brother, Huey, became immediately popular, and Cameron went on to write a whole series of books about them and their friends. Today, readers all over the world know Julian, Huey, Gloria, and Latisha.

Ann Cameron was born on October 21, 1943, in the little town of Rice Lake, Wisconsin. Her father was a lawyer and her mother was a teacher. As a young child, Ann didn't like school very much. She

TO GET HERSELF IN THE MOOD TO WRITE, ANN CAMERON DOES SOMETHING SHE ENJOYS MORE THAN SITTING AT HOME—SHE GOES OUT TO EAT. EVERY SINGLE ONE OF HER BOOKS HAS BEEN WRITTEN IN A RESTAURANT!

preferred being outdoors. Her favorite activities were fishing, riding her pony, and daydreaming about what the land must have been like hundreds of years earlier.

Even though Ann disliked school, she loved reading. Books were a kind of magic to her, and from a very early age she knew she wanted to be a writer when she grew up. That wasn't as easy as she had hoped, however.

First she went to school at Radcliffe College in Massachusetts. Then she got a job with a book publisher in New York City. She went to graduate school at the University of Iowa, attended several writers' conferences, and tried hard to write novels for adults.

It just didn't work. Discouraged, Cameron remembered that children's books are short. Maybe she could write a children's book . . . and she did! *The Seed* was published in 1975, and after that there was no looking back.

"Write what you care about, and the force of your caring will lead you to questioning, imagining, learning—the opening of the heart and mind that lead to the best writing."

Cameron has written many other books besides those about Julian and his friends. *The Secret Life of Amanda K. Woods* is the story of an eleven-year-old girl growing up in Wisconsin. *The Most Beautiful Place in the World* is set in a town in Guatemala that is, well, the most beautiful place in the world. *The Kidnapped Prince: The Life of Olaudah Equiano*

IN 1993, CITY OFFICIALS OF PANAJACHEL, GUATEMALA, CHOSE CAMERON AS THE UNPAID SUPERVISOR OF THE CLOSED TOWN LIBRARY. TODAY, THE LIBRARY HOLDS MORE THAN 3,000 CHILDREN'S BOOKS, AS WELL AS COMPUTERS AND BOOKS ON TAPE.

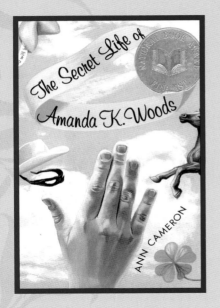

A Selected Bibliography of Cameron's Work

Colibri (2003)

Gloria Rising (2002)

Gloria's Way (2000)

More Stories Huey Tells (1999)

The Secret Life of Amanda K. Woods (1998)

The Kidnapped Prince: The Life of Olaudah Equiano (1995)

The Stories Huey Tells (1995)

Julian, Dream Doctor (1990)

Julian, Secret Agent (1988)

The Most Beautiful Place in the World (1988)

Julian's Glorious Summer (1987)

More Stories Julian Tells (1986)

The Stories Julian Tells (1981)

Harry (The Monster) (1980)

The Angel Book (1977)

The Seed (1975)

tells about a real African child who was captured and sold into slavery in the eighteenth century.

Cameron says her writing has been influenced by living for a long time in a poor country. In 1983, she took what was supposed to be a short vacation to the Central American country of Guatemala. Always eager for new experiences, she soon fell in love with Guatemalan life—and she never really came home. For six years, Cameron divided her time between Guatemala and New York. Then, in 1990, she and her husband, Bill Cherry, decided to live in Guatemala full-time.

Today, Cameron and Cherry live in a small house with flowers growing over the roof, and a view of three volcanoes and a waterfall. They drink fresh lemonade almost every day, made with lemons from their very own lemon tree! Ann Cameron continues

> *"The most important rule for writing is: 'Apply seat of pants to bottom of chair.'"*

to write her own special stories—stories she calls "new thought-flowers blooming in the garden of [my] head."

WHERE TO FIND OUT MORE ABOUT ANN CAMERON

BOOKS

Authors and Artists for Young Adults, Vol. 59. Detroit: Thomson Gale, 2005.

Holtze, Sally Holmes, ed. *Seventh Book of Junior Authors & Illustrators*. New York: H. W. Wilson Company, 1996.

McElmeel, Sharron L. *Bookpeople: A Multicultural Album*. Englewood, Colo.: Teacher Ideas Press, 1992.

WEB SITES

CHILDREN'S BEST BOOKS
http://www.childrensbestbooks.com/
To read more about Ann Cameron's life, to look at her books, and to read answers to questions children frequently ask

HOUGHTON MIFFLIN: MEET THE AUTHOR
http://www.eduplace.com/kids/hmr/mtai/cameron.html
To read a biographical sketch and fun facts about Ann Cameron

WHEN ANN CAMERON WAS GROWING UP, HER FAVORITE PERSON WAS HER GRANDFATHER, OSCAR LOFGREN. HE WAS A BLACKSMITH WHO TAUGHT HER TO SPEAK SWEDISH, TOLD HER STORIES, AND MADE THINGS FOR HER IN HIS BLACKSMITH SHOP.

Eric Carle

Born: June 25, 1929

In the books of Eric Carle, red, yellow, and blue elephants don't fit on a page, caterpillars chew real holes from front to back, fireflies light up with real electric flashbulbs, and the size of each page grows with the size of the animal that lives on it. The animals can often talk, but it is the picture that tells the story. The picture is usually a splash of brilliant color and often includes an animal. It can be found by opening two sides of a page like a door, or flipping pages of different sizes. Sometimes the picture is suspended from the page by a thin strip of paper. And sometimes readers can change around the pictures in the book to make their own story. Thus, the book becomes a toy. What was once a flat, dull page is transformed through texture and color into the vision of Eric Carle.

The creator of *The Very Hungry Caterpillar* and other classic picture books for children was born in

ERIC CARLE'S BOOKS HAVE BEEN TRANSLATED INTO MORE THAN THIRTY LANGUAGES AND HAVE WON PRIZES IN NEW YORK, ITALY, GERMANY, AND JAPAN.

Syracuse, New York, on June 25, 1929. His father, Erich W. Carle, was a civil servant who had come to the United States from Germany with his wife, Johanna Oelschleger Carle.

When Eric was six, his family moved back to their hometown—Stuttgart, Germany. There, he excelled in art classes and was encouraged by his art teachers. During the 1930s, art was an exciting field in Germany. Artists challenged traditional ideas of design and applied their theories to everyday objects. Chairs, forks, spoons, and radios all took on fantastic curving shapes.

But then all that changed. Under the Nazi leadership of Adolf Hitler, Germany entered

A Selected Bibliography of Carle's Work

My Very First Book of Numbers (2006)
Mister Seahorse (2004)
"Slowly, Slowly, Slowly," Said the Sloth (2002)
Does a Kangaroo Have a Mother, Too? (2000)
The Very Clumsy Click Beetle (1999)
From Head to Toe (1997)
The Very Lonely Firefly (1995)
My Apron: A Story from My Childhood (1994)
Today Is Monday (1993)
Draw Me a Star (1992)
The Very Quiet Cricket (1990)
Animals, Animals (1989)
Papa, Please Get the Moon for Me (1986)
The Very Busy Spider (1984)
Let's Paint a Rainbow (1982)
Watch Out! A Giant! (1978)
The Grouchy Ladybug (1977)
Do You Want to Be My Friend? (1971)
The Tiny Seed (1970)
The Very Hungry Caterpillar (1969)
1,2,3 to the Zoo (1968)
Brown Bear, Brown Bear, What Do You See? (Illustrations only, 1967)

Carle's Major Literary Award
2003 Laura Ingalls Wilder Award

a dark period. Artists fled the country. During World War II (1939–1945), Eric's father served in the German army and was held prisoner by the Russians. In the last days of the war, Eric escaped to the countryside to avoid the Allied bombs. These were terrible times—bleak and colorless.

> *"[My father and I] used to go for long walks in the countryside together, and he peeled back tree bark to show me what was underneath it, lift rocks to reveal the insects. As a result, I have an abiding love and affection for small, insignificant animals."*

After the war, Carle studied at the fine arts academy in Stuttgart. He found work designing posters for the U.S. Information Center in Stuttgart. He was on his way to becoming a commercial artist. Carle took his work to New York to find a job. But once in New York, he was drafted into the U.S. Army!

In 1954, Carle married Dorothea Wohlenberg, and the couple had two children. He and Dorothea, however, later divorced, and he married Barbara Morrison in 1973.

In New York, after leaving the army, he was asked to illustrate a children's book. He had never done that before, but by the time he finished, he knew he had found his future profession. He continued to illustrate books for other authors and also began to produce his own.

WHEN ERIC CARLE LEFT GERMANY FOR NEW YORK IN 1952, HE COULD NEVER HAVE IMAGINED HE WOULD BE SENT BACK TO STUTTGART BY THE U.S. ARMY—THIS TIME AS A SOLDIER.

Eric Carle's books teach counting and play with words. Carle says his books are always meant to be fun. Learning will come in time, but he just wants to catch the attention of young readers and spark their imagination.

"I had come to the conclusion that I didn't want to sit in meetings, write memos, entertain clients, and catch commuter trains. I simply wanted to create pictures."

WHERE TO FIND OUT MORE ABOUT ERIC CARLE

BOOKS

Carle, Eric. *Flora and Tiger: 19 Very Short Stories from My Life.* New York: Philomel Books, 1997.

Kovacs, Deborah, and James Preller. *Meet the Authors and Illustrators: 60 Creators of Favorite Children's Books Talk about Their Work.* Vol. 1. New York: Scholastic, 1991.

McElmeel, Sharron L. *100 Most Popular Picture Book Authors and Illustrators: Biographical Sketches and Bibliographies.* Englewood, Colo.: Libraries Unlimited, 2000.

Silvey, Anita, ed. *The Essential Guide to Children's Books and Their Creators.* Boston: Houghton Mifflin Company, 2002.

WEB SITES

ERIC CARLE HOME PAGE
http://www.eric-carle.com/
To read about Eric Carle's life, his books, and frequently asked questions

PICTURE BOOK ART
http://www.picturebookart.org/
For a short biographical sketch and information about the Eric Carle Museum of Picture Book Art

ERIC CARLE IS KNOWN AS THE PIONEER OF THE NOVELTY BOOK. HE WAS ONE OF THE FIRST AUTHORS TO USE FOLD-OUTS, FLASHING LIGHTS, AND COMPUTER CHIPS THAT COULD TALK OR MAKE MUSIC.

Peter Catalanotto

Born: March 21, 1959

Vivid and inviting watercolors are the distinct mark of a book illustrated by Peter Catalanotto. As both an illustrator and an author, Catalanotto brings stories and ideas to life with art as well as words.

Peter Catalanotto was born on March 21, 1959, in Brooklyn, New York, and grew up in a creative household in East Northport, Long Island. From an early age, he spent time drawing, as did most members of his family. In fact, he and three

---

WHEN HE WAS A CHILD, PETER CATALANOTTO ENJOYED DRAWING COMIC-BOOK CHARACTERS. SPIDER-MAN WAS HIS FAVORITE.

of his siblings all attended art schools in New York City.

Catalanotto got his formal art education at the Pratt Institute in Brooklyn, New York, where he earned a bachelor of fine arts degree. While at Pratt, he studied painting and drawing, but Catalanotto soon found that watercolor was the medium he most enjoyed.

> *"I believe a good book doesn't explain everything. It's a springboard, an open door. It gives readers some space to make their own choices and connections."*

After he graduated from Pratt in 1981, Catalanotto got work doing illustrations for newspapers and magazines. Then he began illustrating covers for children's books. After working on the cover of *Just As Long As We're Together,* by Judy Blume, he got a big break. Blume's editor noticed the unique look of Catalanotto's watercolors and offered him the job of illustrating a picture book. This first book for Catalanotto was *All I See,* written by Cynthia Rylant.

> *"One of the things I stress to children in my school presentations is use of their imaginations—to write about what they wished would happen to them along with what really does."*

It wasn't long before Peter Catalanotto began to have story ideas of his own. The first book he wrote and illustrated was *Dylan's Day Out,* a look at a day in the life

CATALANOTTO FAILED TENTH-GRADE ART BECAUSE
HE THOUGHT THE CLASS WAS BORING.

A Selected Bibliography of Catalanotto's Work

Secret Lunch Special (2006)

Kitten Red, Yellow, Blue (2005)

Daisy 1, 2, 3 (2003)

The Dream Shop (Illustrations only, 2002)

Matthew A.B.C. (2002)

Emily's Art (2001)

Book (Illustrations only, 1999)

Dad and Me (1999)

Celebrate!: Stories of the Jewish Holidays (Illustrations only, 1998)

Circle of Thanks (Illustrations only, 1998)

The Rolling Store (Illustrations only, 1997)

A Day at Damp Camp (Illustrations only, 1996)

My House Has Stars (Illustrations only, 1996)

The Painter (1995)

Mama Is a Miner (Illustrations only, 1994)

The Catspring Somersault Flying One-Handed Flip-Flop (1993)

Dreamplace (Illustrations only, 1993)

An Angel for Solomon Singer (Illustrations only, 1992)

Cecil's Story (Illustrations only, 1991)

Christmas Always (1991)

Mr. Mumble (1990)

Soda Jerk (Illustrations only, 1990)

Dylan's Day Out (1989)

Wasted Space (Illustrations only, 1988)

All I See (Illustrations only, 1988)

of a dalmatian. As research for the book, Catalanotto followed his own dog around the house and got to know a dog's world.

In other books, such as *Mr. Mumble,* Catalanotto tackles problems everyone faces, including feeling different, lonely, or left out. As a child, he was often shy and sometimes felt misunderstood by others. He feels it is important to share his experiences with his readers.

> *"As a child I had been strongly impressed by the books I looked at and read, and can still recall those feelings and try to remember them when working."*

Peter Catalanotto con-tinues to illustrate books written by other authors as well as those he has written himself. He lives with his wife, a photographer, and their daughter in Doylestown, Pennsylvania. He enjoys sharing his work with young people by visiting schools and libraries all over the country.

❧

WHERE TO FIND OUT MORE ABOUT PETER CATALANOTTO

BOOKS

Cummings, Pat. *Talking with Artists, Vol. 3: Conversations with Peter Catalanotto, Raul Colon, Lisa Desimini, Jane Dyer, Kevin Hawkes, G. Brian Karas, Betsy Lewin, Ted Lewin, Keiko Narahashi, Elise Primavera, Anna Rich, Peter Sís and Paul O. Zelinsky.* Boston: Houghton Mifflin, 1999.

Holtze, Sally Holmes, ed. *Seventh Book of Junior Authors & Illustrators.* New York: H. W. Wilson Company, 1996.

Silvey, Anita, ed. *The Essential Guide to Children's Books and Their Creators.* Boston: Houghton Mifflin Company, 2002.

Something about the Author. Autobiography Series. Vol. 25. Detroit: Gale Research, 1998.

WEB SITES

VISITINGAUTHORS.COM

http://visitingauthors.com/authors/catalanotto_peter/catalanotto_peter_bio.html
To read an autobiographical sketch and booklist for Peter Catalanotto

―――

THE TITLE OF CATALANOTTO'S *THE PAINTER* APPEARS ON THE BACK OF THE BOOK INSTEAD OF THE FRONT!

John Christopher

(Christopher Samuel Youd)

Born: June 25, 1929

J ohn Christopher is the pseudonym, or pen name, of Christopher Samuel Youd. This prolific author wrote more than fifty books under various names. He is best known for his thrilling science fiction novels for young adults, which he wrote using the name John Christopher.

Christopher Samuel Youd was born in Knowsley, a suburb of Liverpool in Lancashire, England. When he was ten, the family moved to the county of Hampshire. There he attended the Peter Symonds School in Winchester. At the time, it was a boys' grammar school, or secondary school.

As a schoolboy, Christopher loved science and studied physics and chemistry. His science grades were poor,

YOUD USED THE NAME JOHN CHRISTOPHER FOR HIS YOUNG-ADULT SCIENCE FICTION. OTHER PSEUDONYMS INCLUDE CHRISTOPHER YOUD, SAMUEL YOUD, PETER GRAAF, HILARY FORD, PETER NICHOLAS, WILLIAM GODFREY, AND ANTHONY RYE.

though. Abandoning any hope of a science career, he became a fanatic reader of science fiction. He graduated from Peter Symonds School in 1938 at the age of sixteen. While still in his teens, he began publishing a low-budget science fiction magazine called *The Fanatist*. This magazine featured his own articles and short stories. In about 1940, Youd's first professionally published short story appeared in *Liliput* magazine.

After World War II (1939–1945) broke out, Youd enrolled in Great Britain's Royal Signal Corps, where he served from 1941 to 1946. He married Joyce Fairbaim in 1946, and the couple eventually had four daughters and a son.

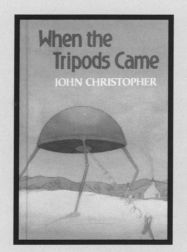

A Selected Bibliography of Christopher's Work

Fireball Trilogy
Dragon Dance (1986)
New Found Land (1983)
Fireball (1981)

Sword of the Sprits Trilogy
The Sword of the Spirits (1972)
Beyond the Burning Lands (1971)
The Prince in Waiting (1970)

Tripods Trilogy
The Pool of Fire (1968)
The City of Gold and Lead (1967)
The White Mountains (1967)

Other Novels
A Dusk of Demons (1994)
When the Tripods Came (1988)
The Guardians (1970)
No Blade of Grass (1956)

> *"What I have learned is that writing for children is at least as exacting and concentration-demanding as writing for adults. . . . It is the form of writing which I can now least imagine giving up."*

In 1949, Youd went to work for an industrial diamond company. On the side, he submitted short stories to science fiction magazines, using the name John Christopher. But short-story writing was not very profitable. He wrote novels furiously at night and on weekends. Sometimes he turned out as many as three books a year. These included thrillers, romance novels, and comedies. For each type of novel, Youd used a different pseudonym. He felt that readers should know what they were getting when they saw a book with a certain author's name.

Youd's first big success was in 1956 with *The Death of Grass*, a science fiction novel for adults. In 1958, he quit his job to write full-time. In the late 1960s, he began writing young-adult novels. This is when he produced his most famous work, the books in the Tripods trilogy. In all three—*The White Mountains*, *The City of Gold and Lead*, and *The Pool of Fire*—Will Parker is the leading character. With great courage, he and his friends save Earth from aliens that occupy the planet.

> *"Freedom of thought is perhaps the greatest good, and needs to be fought for and sacrificed for."*

YOUD'S NOVEL *THE DEATH OF GRASS* WAS LATER GIVEN THE NEW TITLE *NO BLADE OF GRASS*. HIS PUBLISHER THOUGHT THE ORIGINAL TITLE SOUNDED LIKE A GARDENING BOOK. *NO BLADE OF GRASS* WAS MADE INTO A MOVIE IN **1970**.

Youd wrote the Sword of the Spirits trilogy in the early 1970s. These novels take place in a world devastated by natural disasters. Mutants, the victims of solar radiation, are at war with an elite, nonmutant class. A teenager named Luke sets out to unite them in peace. Youd also wrote the Fireball trilogy during the 1980s. Its young heroes are thrust into a parallel reality that takes them back into ancient history.

Youd went on to create many more young-adult novels. He is credited with raising science fiction to a much more sophisticated level than ever before. He now lives in the town of Rye in East Sussex, England.

✿

WHERE TO FIND OUT MORE ABOUT JOHN CHRISTOPHER

BOOKS

Silvey, Anita, ed. *The Essential Guide to Children's Books and Their Creators.* Boston: Houghton Mifflin Company, 2002.

Sutherland, Zena. *Children & Books.* 9th ed. Boston: Allyn & Bacon, 1997.

WEB SITES

ALL SCIENCE FICTION
http://www.allscifi.com/Topic.asp?TopicID=102
For reviews of several of John Christopher's books

THE TRIPODS
http://www.gnelson.demon.co.uk/tripage/jc.html
For a biography and a list of both adult and children's books written by the author

———

THE BRITISH BROADCASTING CORPORATION (BBC) MADE THE TRIPODS TRILOGY INTO A TELEVISION SERIES.

Beverly Cleary

Born: April 12, 1916

When Beverly Cleary first became a writer, she wanted to write books about the kind of kids she remembered in her neighborhood. The books she had read as a child had no funny stories about the sort of children she knew. But all that changed when Cleary published her first book, *Henry Huggins,* in 1950. Since then, she has published dozens of other books including *The Mouse and the Motorcycle, Ramona the Pest,* and *Dear Mr. Henshaw.*

Cleary was born Beverly Bunn, on April 12, 1916, in McMinnville, Oregon. As a young child, Beverly lived on a farm near a small town called Yamhill. Beverly loved to hear the stories her mother told her. She was always asking her mother to read her a book or tell her a story.

BRONZE STATUES OF THREE OF CLEARY'S MOST FAMOUS CHARACTERS—RAMONA QUIMBY, HENRY HUGGINS, AND HENRY'S DOG RIBSY—ARE ON DISPLAY IN THE BEVERLY CLEARY SCULPTURE GARDEN FOR CHILDREN IN PORTLAND, OREGON.

The town they lived in was very small and had no library. Her mother arranged with the state library to have books sent to Yamhill. Beverly's mother set up a small library in a room above the bank. Beverly spent many hours in the library with her mother. She loved to be around books.

When Beverly was six years old, her family moved to Portland, Oregon. She was not used to living in such a big city.

"In this computer age I still write in longhand on yellow paper. Then I type what I have written in my bad typing, revise it, retype it, and take it to a good typist."

A Selected Bibliography of Cleary's Work

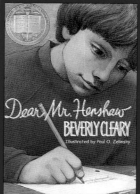

Two Times the Fun (2005)
Lucky Chuck (2002)
Ramona's World (1999)
My Own Two Feet: A Memoir (1995)
Strider (1991)
A Girl from Yamhill: A Memoir (1988)
Ramona Forever (1984)
Dear Mr. Henshaw (1983)
Ralph S. Mouse (1982)
Ramona Quimby, Age 8 (1981)
Ramona and Her Mother (1979)
Ramona and Her Father (1977)
Ramona the Brave (1975)
Runaway Ralph (1970)
Ramona the Pest (1968)
The Mouse and the Motorcycle (1965)
Ribsy (1964)
Henry and the Clubhouse (1962)
Henry and the Paper Route (1957)
Beezus and Ramona (1955)
Henry and Ribsy (1954)
Henry and Beezus (1952)
Ellen Tebbits (1951)
Henry Huggins (1950)

Cleary's Major Literary Awards

1984 Newbery Medal
  Dear Mr. Henshaw

1982 Newbery Honor Book
  Ramona Quimby, Age 8

1981 American Book Award
  Ramona and Her Mother

1978 Boston Globe–Horn Book Fiction Honor Book

1978 Newbery Honor Book
  Ramona and Her Father

1975 Laura Ingalls Wilder Award

> *"I don't believe in outlining works for fiction because if you have it all worked out, it becomes boring. So I just write. I really enjoy revising more than writing. I love to cross things out and cut a page down to one paragraph."*

When she went to first grade, she was put into a group for struggling readers. This was sad and frustrating for her and suddenly she did not like to read anymore.

By the time she entered third grade, however, her love for reading returned. Beverly spent much of her time reading books. She also went to the library often. Her school librarian even told her that she should be a children's author when she grew up. Beverly liked that idea.

After graduating from high school, Beverly Bunn went to California to attend college. She first attended a junior college and then went on to graduate from the University of California at Berkeley. After college, she went to the School of Librarianship at the University of Washington. She took a job as children's librarian at the public library in Yakima, Washington. She worked there until she married Clarence Cleary, and they moved to California.

During World War II (1939–1945), Beverly Cleary worked as the librarian at the Oakland Army Hospital. After the war, Cleary and her husband bought a house. She discovered a pile of blank typing paper in

CLEARY OFTEN WRITES ABOUT TOPICS REQUESTED BY HER READERS. HER BOOKS *DEAR MR. HENSHAW* AND *STRIDER* WERE BASED ON REQUESTS FOR A BOOK ABOUT A BOY WHOSE PARENTS WERE DIVORCED.

the closet of her new home. She decided to use this paper to start her career as a children's author. Her first book, *Henry Huggins,* was published in 1950. She has written numerous other books ranging from picture books to teen novels.

Cleary still lives in California. She continues to write for children and young people.

❧

WHERE TO FIND OUT MORE ABOUT BEVERLY CLEARY

BOOKS

Berg, Julie. *Beverly Cleary.* Edina, Minn.: Abdo & Daughters, 1993.

Cleary, Beverly. *My Own Two Feet: A Memoir.* New York: Morrow, 1995.

Kelly, Joanne. *The Beverly Cleary Handbook.* Englewood, Colo.: Teacher Ideas Press, 1996.

Ward, Stasia. *Meet Beverly Cleary.* New York: PowerKids Press, 2001.

WEB SITES

BEVERLY CLEARY HOME PAGE
http://www.beverlycleary.com
For biographical information on Beverly Cleary, games, and a booklist

EDUCATIONAL PAPERBACK ASSOCIATION
http://edupaperback.org/showauth.cfm?authid=21
To read a biographical sketch and booklist for Beverly Cleary

PORTLAND PARKS AND RECREATION—GRANT PARK
http://www.parks.ci.portland.or.us/Parks/Grant.htm
For information on how to visit bronze statues of Ramona, Henry, and Ribsy in the Beverly Cleary Sculpture Garden for Children in Portland, Oregon

———

JAPANESE, SPANISH, AND SWEDISH TELEVISION PROGRAMS HAVE BEEN BASED ON CLEARY'S HENRY HUGGINS BOOKS. MANY OTHER CLEARY STORIES HAVE ALSO BEEN MADE INTO TELEVISION PROGRAMS.

Vera Cleaver
Bill Cleaver

Born: January 6, 1919 (Vera)   *Died: August 11, 1992 (Vera)*
Born: March 24, 1920 (Bill)   *Died: August 20, 1981 (Bill)*

For fourteen years, Vera and Bill Cleaver worked as a team to create realistic and exciting stories for young adults. They wrote sixteen books together, including some award-winning novels. The most famous book the pair wrote together was *Where the Lilies Bloom.* The novel is about four Appalachian Mountain children who are left to fend for themselves after their mother and father die.

Where the Lilies Bloom won the Cleavers many honors. In 1974, it was made into a movie. Even though the book was written many years ago, people of all ages continue to enjoy it.

———

FOUR OF THE CLEAVERS' NOVELS—*WHERE THE LILIES BLOOM, GROVER, THE WHYS AND WHEREFORES OF LITTABELLE LEE,* AND *QUEEN OF HEARTS*—WERE FINALISTS FOR THE NATIONAL BOOK AWARD.

Vera Fern Allen was born in Virgil, South Dakota, on January 6, 1919, the fifth of nine children. Her family was very poor. William Joseph Cleaver was born in Hugo, Oklahoma, on March 24, 1920. After Bill's parents divorced, he was sent to a private school in British Columbia, Canada. At the start of World War II (1939–1945), Bill joined the U.S. Army Air Corps. He and Vera met during the war.

Vera and Bill had a special bond: they both loved reading and learning. As teenagers, both Bill and Vera immersed themselves in the world of books and learning. They spent hour after hour at public libraries, reading

"When the characters and the plot are clear and defined, they practically dictate the words to me."
—Vera Cleaver

one book after another. Both Vera and Bill also loved writing. Vera wrote her first story at the age of six. Her grandfather, a newspaper publisher, helped her. Bill wrote as a child, too. He knew that he would be a writer one day.

Vera and Bill married in 1945. They lived in Japan and France before settling down in Florida. The two began their writing careers together by creating more than 300 fiction stories for magazines. Later, they published articles in magazines such as *McCall's* and *Woman's Day.* Finally, though, they decided that they wanted to write fiction for children.

———

THE CLEAVERS' BOOKS ARE SET IN MANY DIFFERENT LOCATIONS, INCLUDING THE APPALACHIAN MOUNTAINS, THE OZARK MOUNTAINS, CHICAGO, SEATTLE, AND SOUTH DAKOTA.

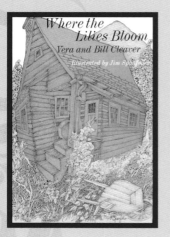

A Selected Bibliography of the Cleavers' Work

Belle Pruitt (1988)
Moon Lake Angel: A Novel (1987)
Hazel Rye (1983)
The Kissimmee Kid (1981)
A Little Destiny (1979)
Queen of Hearts (1978)
Trial Valley (1977)
Dust of the Earth (1975)
Me Too (1973)
The Whys and Wherefores of Littabelle Lee (1973)
Delpha Green & Company (1972)
I Would Rather Be a Turnip (1971)
The Mock Revolt (1971)
The Mimosa Tree (1970)
Grover (1970)
Where the Lilies Bloom (1969)
Lady Ellen Grae (1968)
Ellen Grae (1967)

The Cleavers' Major Literary Award

1970 Boston Globe–Horn Book Fiction Honor Book
  Where the Lilies Bloom

How did this husband-and-wife team work? First, the pair brainstormed an idea together. They talked and talked about the idea for months. Then Bill researched the idea. He learned as much as he could about the time and place of the story. Finally, Vera sat down and began to write the story. She did all the actual writing.

Vera and Bill created realistic teen characters and then placed them into a seriously sticky situation. Their characters had to use their wits to overcome their problems. In their

> *"We wouldn't trade being what we are for anything."*
> —Bill Cleaver

books, the Cleavers never avoided sensitive topics. They tackled suicide, the death of a parent, caring for the elderly, and other hardships. Even though the issues were often somber, Bill and Vera managed to keep their novels from being depressing. To help, Vera kept a note from Bill next to her typewriter. The note said, "Don't be so serious."

In 1981, Bill Cleaver died in Florida at the age of sixty-one. Vera continued to write without him, penning several books on her own, including *Sweetly Sings the Donkey.* Vera Cleaver died in Florida in 1992.

❧

WHERE TO FIND OUT MORE ABOUT VERA AND BILL CLEAVER

BOOKS

Chevalier, Tracy, ed. *Twentieth-Century Children's Writers.* 3rd ed. Chicago: St. James Press, 1989.

Sutherland, Zena. *Children and Books.* 9th ed. New York: Addison Wesley Longman, 1997.

Twentieth-Century Young Adult Writers. Detroit: St. James Press, 1994.

WEB SITE

HARPER CHILDRENS
http://www.harperchildrens.com/catalog/author_xml.asp?authorid=11931
For biographical information and booklist

―――――

AFTER HE LEFT THE U.S. ARMY, BILL CLEAVER WORKED
AS A JEWELER AND WATCHMAKER FOR FOUR YEARS.

Andrew Clements

Born: May 29, 1949

Books have always been an important part of Andrew Clements's life. He was a teacher of English and reading. He had many jobs in the book publishing industry including salesperson and editor. His love of books led him to become a well-known author of books for children and young people. Clements's best-known books include *Double Trouble in Walla Walla, Frindle, Who Owns the Cow?* and *Hey Dad, Could I Borrow Your Hammer?* Clements has also written reading program books for schools.

Clements was born on May 29, 1949, in Camden, New Jersey. His family lived first in New Jersey and then moved to Illinois. Andrew knew how to

---

ONE OF CLEMENTS'S JOBS IN THE PUBLISHING INDUSTRY WAS TO TRANSLATE AND ADAPT EUROPEAN PICTURE BOOKS FOR THE UNITED STATES MARKET.

read when he started kindergarten. His parents enjoyed reading and always had books around the house.

Andrew loved to go to the library at school. He chose a large book on myths on his first visit to the school library. When he brought the book back the next day, the librarian thought he was returning it because it was too difficult. The librarian was surprised when Andrew told her that he had already finished the book. He wanted another book! "That event created for me an open invitation to head to the library just about any old time I wanted to," Andrew Clements says. "And the librarian was a gem. She kept me well stocked."

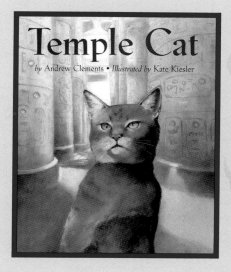

A Selected Bibliography of Clements's Work

Slippers Love to Run (2006)
Lunch Money (2005)
Report Card (2004)
The Jacket (2002)
Jake Drake, Teacher's Pet (2002)
Brave Norman: A True Story (2001)
Jake Drake, Bully Buster (2001)
The Janitor's Boy (2000)
Hey Dad, Could I Borrow Your Hammer? (1999)
The Laundry News (1999)
Life in the Desert (1998)
Double Trouble in Walla Walla (1997)
Bright Christmas: An Angel Remembers (1996)
Frindle (1996)
A Dog's Best Friend (1995)
Who Owns the Cow? (1995)
Temple Cat (1991)
Santa's Secret Helper (1990)
Big Al (1988)

"One of the few places on earth that it is still possible to experience an instant sense of freedom and privacy is anywhere we open up a good book and begin to read."

Andrew Clements was also a good writer. As a high school student, his English teacher asked him to write a parody. The teacher loved his work and thought it was very funny. She praised Andrew for his writing talent and encouraged him to become a writer.

When Clements entered Northwestern University, he studied English and writing. He took many creative writing classes and wrote poems and song lyrics.

After finishing college in 1972, Clements took a job as a teacher. He worked as a teacher for seven years at both elementary and high schools. "As a teacher, it was a thrill to read a book aloud, and see a whole class listen so carefully to every word, dying to know what would happen next," Clements says. "And I was amazed at the wonderful discussions a good book can spark."

Clements then began working in the publishing industry. He worked at several different publishing jobs before he decided

"The way I really got started writing was by reading. Before too long I found myself reading something good and saying to myself, 'I wish I had written that!'"

CLEMENTS'S NOVEL *FRINDLE* WAS WRITTEN FOR MIDDLE-SCHOOL STUDENTS. THE BOOK HAS BEEN NOMINATED FOR MORE THAN THIRTY-FIVE AWARDS ACROSS THE UNITED STATES.

to write his own book. He went on to write picture books for children and fiction books for young adults. Clements has won many awards for his writing.

Clements lives in Westborough, Massachusetts, with his family. He continues to write books for children and young people. He also travels throughout the United States visiting schools.

&

WHERE TO FIND OUT MORE ABOUT ANDREW CLEMENTS

BOOKS

Rockman, Connie C., ed. *Eighth Book of Junior Authors and Illustrators.* New York: H. W. Wilson Company, 2000.

Silvey, Anita, ed. *The Essential Guide to Children's Books and Their Creators.* Boston: Houghton Mifflin Company, 2002.

Something about the Author. Vol. 104. Detroit: Gale Research, 1999.

WEB SITES

ANDREW CLEMENTS HOME PAGE
http://andrewclements.com/
For the author's web site with biographical information, booklists, news, and more

HOUGHTON MIFFLIN: MEET THE AUTHOR
http://www.eduplace.com/kids/hmr/mtai/clements.html
To read a biographical sketch and booklist for Andrew Clements

---

CLEMENTS COVERS MANY THEMES IN HIS PICTURE BOOKS. THEIR SUBJECTS RANGE FROM LEARNING HOW TO COUNT TO ACCEPTING DIFFERENCES IN PEOPLE.

Brock Cole

Born: May 29, 1938

Brock Cole is one of those amazing people who can both write and illustrate books. He is the creator of such terrific (and terrifically different) books as *The Goats, The Giant's Toe, Buttons,* and *The Facts Speak for Themselves.* But the funny thing is, Cole didn't

start out to be either a writer or an illustrator.

Brock Cole was born in the little town of Charlotte, Michigan, on May 29, 1938. His family moved around a lot when he was a child, but Brock didn't mind. He considered himself an explorer. Some of his favorite times were spent roaming the woodlots, creeks,

BROCK COLE'S PICTURE BOOKS AND NOVELS HAVE WON JUST ABOUT EVERY AWARD GIVEN FOR CHILDREN'S BOOKS. ONE CRITIC SAID THAT HIS FIRST YOUNG-ADULT NOVEL, *THE GOATS*, WAS "ONE OF THE MOST IMPORTANT BOOKS OF THE DECADE."

lakes, backstreets, and alleys of his various neighborhoods. Wherever Brock's family lived, the first thing he looked for was the local library.

In time, Brock Cole graduated from high school, went to college, and started a career as a teacher. First he taught writing courses in college. Then he switched to philosophy courses. And then he got tired of teaching. What he really wanted to do was create books for children.

> *"To be honest, I simply tag along after [my wife] Susan. It's her [academic] research that takes us all over the place. I enjoy it immensely, though. There's something about sitting down to work at a rickety table in a strange city that clears the head. It's the best thing for a writer, or for this one, anyway."*

Cole already knew a lot about writing, but he knew nothing about illustrating. And since he knew his stories needed pictures, he decided to teach himself to draw. He studied other artists whose work he liked. He practiced and practiced. And, in 1979, he was ready to publish his very first picture book, *The King at the Door: Words and Pictures.*

Cole's picture books are full of color, wit, and humor. He tells stories about fairy-tale families and conceited pigs and little girls who hate baths. Each book is completely different from the one that came before it.

———

COLE REMEMBERS HIS CHILDHOOD HOME IN CHARLOTTE, MICHIGAN, AS BEING "A PLACE WHERE A SIX-YEAR-OLD COULD WANDER INTO THE FEED MILL OR THE AUTO-BODY SHOP AND WATCH MEN WORK WITHOUT BEING CHASED OUT."

A Selected Bibliography of Cole's Work

George Washington's Teeth (Illustrations only, 2003)
Larky Mavis (2001)
Buttons (2000)
The Facts Speak for Themselves (1997)
Alpha and the Dirty Baby (1991)
Celine (1989)
The Goats (1987)
The Giant's Toe (1986)
Gaffer Samson's Luck (Illustrations only, 1984)
The Winter Wren (1984)
Nothing but a Pig (1981)
No More Baths (1980)
The Indian in the Cupboard (Illustrations only, 1980)
The King at the Door: Words and Pictures (1979)

Cole's Major Literary Award

2000 Boston Globe–Horn Book Picture Book Honor Book
  Buttons

Cole has also written full-length novels for older children and teenagers. These books are set firmly in our modern world and deal with serious subjects. The main characters find out that other kids can be cruel, adults can be stupid, and life can be scary. But Cole's young protagonists are smart, resourceful, and frequently funny. They face their problems squarely and never give up on themselves. They are survivors.

"I had always wanted to write, and I loved to draw. I had small children, who were a wonderful audience. Children's books seemed a perfect fit."

Cole and his wife, Susan, have two grown sons and one grandson. They live in Oak Park, Illinois, but they love to travel. They especially enjoy spending their summers in Greece or Turkey. And who knows— maybe that's where Cole's next book idea will come from.

❧

WHERE TO FIND OUT MORE ABOUT BROCK COLE

BOOKS

Children's Literature Review. Vol. 18.
Detroit: Gale Research, 1989.

Holtze, Sally Holmes, ed. *Sixth Book of Junior Authors & Illustrators.*
New York: H. W. Wilson Company, 1989.

St. James Guide to Young Adult Writers. 2nd ed. Detroit: St. James Press, 1999.

Silvey, Anita, ed. *The Essential Guide to Children's Books and Their Creators.*
Boston: Houghton Mifflin Company, 2002.

WEB SITES

FRONT STREET BOOKS
http://www.frontstreetbooks.com/all_books.htm
To read a biographical sketch and booklist for Brock Cole

EDUCATIONAL PAPERBACK ASSOCIATION
http://www.edupaperback.org/showauth2.cfm?authid=123
To read a biographical sketch

SOMETIMES COLE ILLUSTRATES BOOKS WRITTEN BY OTHER AUTHORS. HE DREW THE PICTURES FOR *THE INDIAN IN THE CUPBOARD* BY LYNNE REID BANKS (1980) AND FOR *GAFFER SAMSON'S LUCK* BY JILL PATON WALSH (1984).

Joanna Cole

Born: August 11, 1944

There's a little bit of Ms. Frizzle, the wildly dressed teacher and star of the Magic School Bus series, in author Joanna Cole herself. The character, based on Joanna's favorite elementary-school science teacher, has the same love of science and children that motivated Cole to write for young readers.

Joanna Cole was born on August 11, 1944, in Newark, New Jersey. As a child, she was fascinated by gardening, insects, and animals. She was always curious about how and why things are the way they are. She also loved reading children's books, an interest that carried over into her adult life.

In school, English and science were Joanna's best subjects. Writing about science turned out to be a perfect way to combine these interests. "As a child, I enjoyed writing and I

JOANNA COLE DID SOME OF THE RESEARCH FOR HER FIRST BOOK, *COCKROACHES,* IN HER NEW YORK CITY APARTMENT, WHERE MANY OF THE CREATURES SCAMPERED AROUND RIGHT BEFORE HER EYES!

wrote for the sheer fun of it. I think that's very important—not to be always looking at what the outside world will say about you," says Cole.

After finishing high school in East Orange, New Jersey, Cole attended the University of Massachusetts and Indiana University. She finally graduated from the City College of New York with a bachelor's degree in psychology.

After college, Cole worked as a librarian in a Brooklyn elementary school, followed by a period as an elementary schoolteacher. Her first writing job was at *Newsweek* magazine. There, she answered letters to the editor.

During her years as an elementary-school librarian, Joanna Cole rediscovered her love of children's books. She left the academic world and took a job at Doubleday Books for Young Readers. After eventually working her way up to the position of senior editor, she decided to try her own hand at writing children's books. Realizing that very few books for kids are about insects—and none at all are about the dreaded cockroach—Cole began research for her first published book, *Cockroaches*.

From there, she tackled such subjects as plants, dinosaurs, frogs, horses, and cats. When an editor at Scholastic suggested that Cole

> *"I had a teacher who was a little like Ms. Frizzle. She loved her subject. Every week she had a child do an experiment in front of the room, and I wanted to be that child every week!"*

COLE ALWAYS CREATES A "DUMMY" MAGIC SCHOOL BUS BOOK WITH TEXT, WORD BALLOONS, ROUGH SKETCHES, AND JOKES ON SMALL STICK-ON NOTES. WHEN SHE MEETS WITH HER EDITOR, COLE PEELS OFF THE NOTES TO FIND THE JOKES THAT MAKE HER EDITOR LAUGH.

A Selected Bibliography of Cole's Work

Ms. Fizzle's Adventures: Imperial China (2005)

Ms. Fizzle's Adventures: Medieval Castle (2002)

Ms. Frizzle's Adventures: Ancient Egypt (2001)

Gator Halloween (1999)

Get Well, Gators! (1998)

The Magic School Bus in the Rain Forest (1998)

I'm a Big Brother (1997)

The Magic School Bus: Inside a Beehive (1996)

How I Was Adopted: Samantha's Story (1995)

The Magic School Bus Gets Baked in a Cake: A Book about Kitchen Chemistry (1995)

The Magic School Bus on the Ocean Floor (1992)

The Magic School Bus, Lost in the Solar System (1990)

The Magic School Bus: Inside the Earth (1987)

The Magic School Bus at the Waterworks (1986)

How You Were Born (1984)

Bony-Legs (1983)

A Frog's Body (1980)

My Puppy Is Born (1973)

Cockroaches (1971)

Cole's Major Literary Award

1987 Boston Globe–Horn Book Nonfiction Honor Book
  The Magic School Bus at the Waterworks

combine science with fictional characters, the award-winning Magic School Bus series was born. Covering subjects such as the solar system, the weather, the ocean floor, and bees, the hugely popular series is well respected by educators and experts alike.

The books led to an animated series on PBS television. Students can also visit a

"We all learn to be writers from the books we read as kids. Reading gives you a very solid feel for the language, and an understanding of how to write. When you start to write, you can use that understanding."

Magic School Bus Web site to explore many topics in a fun-filled way with the Magic School Bus gang.

Readers of the Magic School Bus series, with colorful illustrations by Bruce Degen, know that Joanna Cole has a great sense of humor, as well as a thorough scientific knowledge. So it comes as no surprise that she has recently written a series of humor books. She has also authored a collection of folktales from around the world. But readers know Joanna Cole best as the real-life counterpart to everyone's favorite frizzy-haired teacher.

❦

WHERE TO FIND OUT MORE ABOUT JOANNA COLE

BOOKS

Cole, Joanna. *On the Bus with Joanna Cole: A Creative Autobiography.*
Portsmouth, N.H.: Heinemann, 1996.

Silvey, Anita, ed. *The Essential Guide to Children's Books and Their Creators.*
Boston: Houghton Mifflin Company, 2002.

WEB SITES

EDUCATIONAL PAPERBACK ASSOCIATION
http://edupaperback.org/showauth.cfm?authid=22
To read a biographical sketch and booklist for Joanna Cole

KIDSREADS.COM
http://www.kidsreads.com/authors/au-cole-joanna.asp
To read an autobiographical account of Joanna Cole

MAGIC SCHOOL BUS WEB SITE FROM SCHOLASTIC
http://www.scholastic.com/magicschoolbus/home.htm
For games and an art gallery related to the popular television series

———

IT TAKES ABOUT A YEAR FOR JOANNA COLE TO WRITE A MAGIC SCHOOL BUS BOOK. SHE SPENDS SIX MONTHS ON RESEARCH AND SIX MONTHS ON WRITING.

Eoin Colfer

Born: May 14, 1965

By now, a lot of people know that Eoin Colfer's first name is pronounced "Owen." That's because his Artemis Fowl books are international best sellers. Aimed at a young audience, these fantasy and science fiction thrillers are choice reading for adults, too.

Eoin Colfer was born in Wexford, Ireland, in 1965. He was the second oldest of five boys. His father was a schoolteacher at Wexford's Christian Brothers' Primary School for boys. He was also an artist and historian. Eoin's mother was a drama teacher, actress, and playwright. Both parents encouraged him to explore his creativity.

Eoin attended the school where his father taught. In sixth grade, he wrote his first story—complete with illustrations. It was about the Vikings in Norse mythology, and

---

**COLFER DISLIKES STINKY FOODS SUCH AS ONIONS AND GARLIC.
HE ALSO DISLIKES IRONING CLOTHES.**

the characters were Eoin and his friends. The plot left everyone except Eoin dead at the end of the story.

At age twelve, he entered the Christian Brothers' secondary school in Wexford. It offered a six-year course of study. In the fifth year, the boys were allowed to attend dances at the local girls' school. There Eoin met a girl named Jackie. "She had great spiked hair and blue eyeliner," he says. The two became sweethearts.

As a teenager, Eoin didn't quite fit in with other boys in the neighborhood because he was small and not very good at sports. He spent his time tracing pictures of fairies from books about Ireland's Celtic folklore.

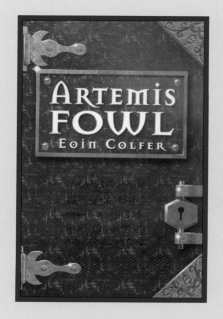

A Selected Bibliography of Colfer's Work

Half-Moon Investigations (2006)
Artemis Fowl: The Opal Deception (2005)
The Legend of Captain Crow's Teeth (2005)
Artemis Fowl Files (2004)
The Legend of Spud Murphy (2004)
The Supernaturalist (2004)
Artemis Fowl: The Eternity Code (2003)
Artemis Fowl: The Arctic Incident (2002)
Artemis Fowl (2001)
Ed's Bed (2001)
Ed's Funny Feet (2000)
The Wish List (2000)
Benny and Babe (1999)
Going Potty (1999)
Benny and Omar (1998)

> "[As a child,] I was into fairies with axes; I was never into them flitting round the garden."

But the fairies he liked were not the delicate type. As he later explained, "The fairies of Irish mythology are . . . very warlike. Always up for a fight."

Colfer finished secondary school in 1983. Then he took a three-year teachers' training course in Dublin, Ireland. After graduating in 1986, he began teaching elementary school back in Wexford. In 1991, he and Jackie got married. The couple spent four years teaching in Saudi Arabia, Tunisia, and Italy. Returning to Wexford, they continued teaching and eventually had two sons, Finn and Sean.

Colfer kept writing, too. His first book, *Benny and Omar*, was published in 1998. After writing five more children's books, he began the Artemis Fowl series. The hero, Artemis Fowl, is a brilliant criminal mastermind—and he's only twelve years old. Greedy for wealth, he decides to prey on the underground world of "the People"—a land of fairies, pixies, and dwarfs. The two sides engage in many power struggles, matching wits and fighting action-packed battles.

> "My own pupils were a fantastic help to me when I began writing. They gave me general ideas and specific one-liners every day. Some even made it into the books."

IT TAKES COLFER ABOUT SIX TO NINE MONTHS TO WRITE A BOOK.

Artemis Fowl, the first book in the series, came out in 2001. Even before it was released, movie companies were bargaining fiercely for the rights to the manuscript. As expected, *Artemis Fowl* was a huge success. Financially secure, Colfer was able to quit his teaching job in 2001. This also gave him time to travel on promotional tours.

Occasionally taking a break from Artemis, Colfer has written stories about the hilarious yet dangerous adventures of two brothers named Will and Marty. Another Artemis Fowl book, as well as a movie, is expected in 2007. Colfer still lives in Wexford with his wife and two sons.

WHERE TO FIND OUT MORE ABOUT EOIN COLFER

WEB SITES
ARTEMIS FOWL
http://www.artemisfowl.com/
To read about the Artemis Fowl series and information about the author as well as reviews of his books

EOIN COLFER
http://www.eoincolfer.com/
For a Web site devoted to the author

O'BRIEN PRESS
http://www.obrien.ie/author.cfm?authorid=130
For a biography and links to interviews

COLFER COFOUNDED THE WEXFORD BOOK FESTIVAL. IT'S A FOUR-DAY EVENT WITH AUTHOR APPEARANCES, BOOK SIGNINGS, COMPETITIONS, AND WORKSHOPS.

Bryan Collier

Born: January 31, 1967

B ryan Collier might have become a football player. But he chose another path—art. Now he illustrates picture books for children with his bold, vivid images.

Born in Salisbury, Maryland, in 1967, Bryan Collier grew up in Pocomoke, Maryland, on the eastern shore of Chesapeake Bay. He was the youngest of six children. When he began reading, he liked the stories, but he especially liked the illustrations.

Bryan began painting when he was fifteen. He painted all he saw around him—the bay, the ducks, and the marshes. At first, he used only watercolors, but he began to develop a unique style. It combined watercolors and collage, a technique that involves gluing objects onto a picture's surface. Bryan cut out photos from magazines and incorporated them into his paintings.

IN THE 1990s, COLLIER DIRECTED A PROGRAM FOR KIDS IN NEW YORK CITY'S HARLEM THAT GAVE THEM THE OPPORTUNITY TO CREATE HUGE WALL PAINTINGS CALLED MURALS.

When Bryan was a senior in high school, he entered the 1985 Congressional Art Competition, a nationwide contest for high-school artists. Collier won first place in his district, and his work was exhibited in the Capitol in Washington, D.C. That same year, he received a scholarship to study art at the Pratt Institute in New York City.

> *"For me, [working with children is] almost a ministry in which I can talk to kids about who they really are."*

Bryan was also a talented football player, and recruiters were talking to him about joining their college football teams. It was tempting, but deep down, he knew he wanted to go to New York and be an artist. "It was a scary decision," he says. At the last minute, he decided against football and chose art.

At the Pratt Institute, Collier majored in painting. He graduated with honors in 1989. While at Pratt, he also began volunteering in New York City's Harlem neighborhood. He worked for the Harlem Horizon Art Studio at the Harlem Hospital Center. This program helps seriously injured kids to heal through painting and drawing. After college, Collier was the program's director for twelve years.

In the mid-1990s, Collier was looking at children's books in a bookstore. As he recalls, "I saw books that didn't look or feel or sound like me or my kids or my people." He was determined to fill that gap.

A MURAL PAINTED BY COLLIER APPEARED IN A 1992 *SESAME STREET* EPISODE ABOUT SPEEDY VAN GO, THE FASTEST PAINTER IN THE WORLD.

A Selected Bibliography of Collier's Work

Welcome, Precious (2006)

Rosa (2005)

John's Secret Dreams: The Life of John Lennon (2004)

What's the Hurry, Fox? (2004)

I'm Your Child, God (2002)

Kiss It Up to God (2002)

Visiting Langston (2002)

Jump at the Sun Treasury (2001)

Martin's Big Words: The Life of Dr. Martin Luther King, Jr. (2001)

Freedom River (2000)

Uptown (Text and illustrations, 2000)

These Hands (1999)

Collier's Major Literary Awards

2006 Caldecott Honor Book
2006 Coretta Scott King Illustrator Award
   Rosa

2003 Coretta Scott King Illustrator Honor Book
   Visiting Langston

2002 Caldecott Honor Book
2002 Coretta Scott King Illustrator Honor Book
2002 Orbis Pictus Honor Book
   Martin's Big Words: The Life of Dr. Martin Luther King, Jr.

2001 Coretta Scott King Illustrator Honor Book
   Freedom River

2001 Coretta Scott King Illustrator Award
   Uptown

He got his chance in 1999, illustrating *These Hands*, by Hope Lynne Price. It's about a little African American girl discovering all she can do with her hands.

The next year, Collier published *Uptown*, his first illustrated book using his own text. It's about a boy in Harlem and helps readers experience the neighborhood's sights, sounds, and feelings. Collier went on to illustrate books about African American poet Langston

"In my art and in my life I'm looking for the thread that connects all of us and I'm looking for that seed of individuality."

Hughes, civil rights pioneers Rosa Parks and Martin Luther King, and many other famous people.

For his collages, Collier still cuts pictures from old magazines. He often makes bizarre connections and sees things that aren't obvious to other people. In one magazine, for example, he saw a close-up of a barbecued chicken. Collier realized at once how he could use it in his art: "That was . . . the greatest jacket that you can imagine."

Collier now lives and works in Harlem. He enjoys visiting classrooms and libraries throughout the country.

❧

WHERE TO FIND OUT MORE ABOUT BRYAN COLLIER

BOOKS
Silvey, Anita, ed. *The Essential Guide to Children's Books and Their Creators.* Boston: Houghton Mifflin Company, 2002.

WEB SITES
BRYAN COLLIER
http://www.bryancollier.com/
For a Web site dedicated to the illustrator

HYPERION BOOKS FOR CHILDREN
http://www.hyperionbooksforchildren.com/authors/displayAI.asp?id=16&ai=i
For a short biography and a list of books

SCHOOL LIBRARY JOURNAL
http://www.schoollibraryjournal.com/index.asp?layout=article&articleid= CA73650&publication=slj
To read an interview from 2001

———

COLLIER'S MURALS WERE FEATURED IN THE 1992 BASKETBALL MOVIE *ABOVE THE RIM*, STARRING TUPAC SHAKUR AND MARLON WAYANS.

James Lincoln Collier
Christopher Collier

Born: June 27, 1928 (James)
Born: January 29, 1930 (Christopher)

James Lincoln Collier (pictured below left) and Christopher Collier (pictured below right) are not the only writers in their family. Their father wrote fiction and children's books, an uncle was a novelist, and some of their cousins are journalists. James Lincoln Collier writes

historical fiction and nonfiction books for young people with his brother, Christopher. The brothers' best-known books for young people include *My Brother Sam Is Dead, War Comes to Willy Freeman,* and *With Every Drop of Blood.*

James Lincoln Collier was born on June 27, 1928, in New York City. Because he had so many writers in his family, he knew he wanted to become a writer. After serving

---

JAMES LINCOLN COLLIER PLAYS THE TROMBONE FOR
A JAZZ BAND IN NEW YORK CITY.

in the army for two years, he moved back to New York City. He struggled to find work as a writer and finally took a job as a magazine editor. After about six years, he began to sell his writing to magazines and book publishers. His first nonfiction children's book, *Battleground: The United States Army in World War II,* was published in 1965. He went on to write books about historical events, music, and musicians as well as fiction books for young people.

Christopher Collier was born on January 29, 1930, in New York City. As a young boy, he loved writing. He also became so interested in American history that he went to college and studied that subject. He is

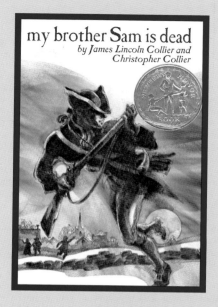

A Selected Bibliography of the Colliers' Work

Middle Road: American Politics, 1945–2000 (2002)
United States in the Cold War, 1945–1989 (2002)
Wild Boy (James Lincoln Collier only, 2002)
The Changing Face of America, 1945–2000 (2001)
World War Two (2001)
The Rise of the Cities, 1820–1920 (2000)
Andrew Jackson's America, 1824–1850 (1999)
The American Revolution, 1763–1783 (1998)
With Every Drop of Blood (1994)
The Clock (1992)
Who Is Carrie? (1984)
War Comes to Willy Freeman (1983)
Jump Ship to Freedom (1981)
My Brother Sam Is Dead (1974)
Battle Ground: The United States Army in World War II (James Lincoln Collier only, 1965)

The Colliers' Major Literary Awards

1975 Newbery Honor Book
   My Brother Sam Is Dead

especially interested in the Revolutionary War (1775–1783). Christopher has worked as a history teacher and professor for many years. He has also written about historical events for adults. He did not write for children until he suggested to his brother, James, that they work together on a children's book.

In 1974, the Collier brothers published

> *"I am very leery of the term 'artist.' I think of myself as a professional, a craftsman, and I believe that if there is anything such as art, it is the residue of craft."*
> —James Lincoln Collier

> *"Most of the writing I do helps other historians learn about the past. But grown-ups are very hard to teach new things to, so I suspect that the writing I do for kids really is more effective."*
> —Christopher Collier

their first book—*My Brother Sam Is Dead*. They went on to write several other historical fiction books. Because Christopher studies the Revolutionary War as a historian, most of their books are set during the war. The brothers have also written more than twenty nonfiction books for a series called Drama of American History.

The Collier brothers divide the tasks when they write a book together. First, Christopher thinks of an idea for a book. Then he researches the related details and information. He makes sure that the facts used

CHRISTOPHER COLLIER WAS NOMINATED FOR A PULITZER PRIZE IN 1971 FOR A BOOK FOR ADULTS, *ROGER SHERMAN'S CONNECTICUT: YANKEE POLITICS AND THE AMERICAN REVOLUTION.*

in the books are accurate. Using Christopher's research, James writes the story and creates the book's characters. Along with telling an interesting story, the Collier brothers also want to help readers learn about history.

James Lincoln Collier lives in New York and continues to write fiction and nonfiction books for young people. Christopher Collier, now a professor of history, lives in Connecticut. The brothers continue to write books together.

WHERE TO FIND OUT MORE ABOUT JAMES LINCOLN COLLIER AND CHRISTOPHER COLLIER

BOOKS

Collier, Laurie, and Joyce Nakamura, eds. *Major Authors and Illustrators for Children and Young Adults.* Detroit: Gale Research, 1993.

McElmeel, Sharron L. *100 Most Popular Children's Authors: Biographical Sketches and Bibliographies.* Englewood, Colo.: Libraries Unlimited, 1999.

Sutherland, Zena. *Children & Books.* 9th ed. New York: Addison Wesley Longman, 1997.

WEB SITE

EDUCATIONAL PAPERBACK ASSOCIATION
http://edupaperback.org/showauth.cfm?authid=49
To read an autobiographical sketch and booklist for James Lincoln Collier

RANDOM HOUSE
http://www.randomhouse.com/author/results.pperl?authorid=5394
For biographical information about James Lincoln Collier

CHRISTOPHER COLLIER BECAME INTERESTED IN WRITING BOOKS FOR CHILDREN BECAUSE MOST OF THE HISTORY BOOKS HE READ WERE NOT VERY INTERESTING. HE WANTED TO MAKE HISTORY COME ALIVE FOR YOUNG PEOPLE.

Barbara Cooney

*Born: August 6, 1917
Died: March 10, 2000*

I t's hard to know where to begin when writing about an author and artist like Barbara Cooney. Cooney was born on August 6, 1917, and died on March 10, 2000. She wrote and illustrated more than one hundred children's books over a gloriously productive sixty-year career.

Barbara Cooney was born in Brooklyn, New York. Her family moved when she was just two weeks old. Barbara lived in Long Island during the school year and spent the summers in Maine. Barbara and her three brothers loved Maine best.

Young Barbara always knew she would be an artist of some sort. It was in her blood—her great-grandfather, her grandmother, and her mother were all artists. As a child, she was allowed to use her mother's art supplies—as long as she kept the brushes clean!

BARBARA COONEY HAD A TWIN BROTHER.

Barbara Cooney studied art and art history at Smith College in Northampton, Massachusetts. Then she packed up her portfolio of artwork and went to New York City to see if she could make a career for herself in children's books. She could! In 1940, she illustrated *Åke and His World,* written by the Swedish poet Bertil Malmberg. The next year she wrote and illustrated her own *King of Wreck Island.*

> *"I was no more talented than any other child. I started out ruining the wallpaper with crayons, like everybody else, and making eggs with arms and legs."*

Barbara Cooney's career as a children's book author and illustrator was interrupted by World War II (1939–1945). In 1942, she joined the Women's Army Corps. Later that same year, she married Guy Murchie. They had two children—Gretel and Barnaby. Barbara and Guy divorced in 1947. Two years later, Cooney married a doctor named C. Talbot Porter. They had two children, Talbot Jr. and Phoebe.

By this time, Barbara Cooney was writing and illustrating several books a year. Although Cooney always said that her first love was color, she did many of her earliest books in black and white.

Whether she was drawing in black and white or in color, however, Barbara Cooney always insisted on accuracy and detail. She drew what she knew—plants from her garden, a neighbor's chickens, her own children and

----

BARBARA COONEY LOVED MAINE—AND MAINE LOVED BARBARA. IN 1996, GOVERNMENT OFFICIALS NAMED BARBARA COONEY AN OFFICIAL STATE TREASURE!

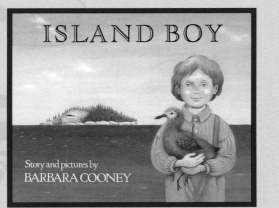

A Selected Bibliography of Cooney's Work

Basket Moon (Illustrations only, 1999)

Eleanor (1996)

Only Opal: The Diary of a Young Girl (Illustrations only, 1994)

Animal Folk Songs for Children: Traditional American Songs (Illustrations only, 1993)

Emily (Illustrations only, 1992)

Letting Swift River Go (Illustrations only, 1992)

Roxaboxen (Illustrations only, 1991)

Hattie and the Wild Waves: A Story from Brooklyn (1990)

Island Boy: Story and Pictures (1988)

The Year of the Perfect Christmas Tree: An Appalachian Story (Illustrations only, 1988)

The Story of Holly and Ivy (Illustrations only, 1985)

Miss Rumphius (1982)

Ox-Cart Man (Illustrations only, 1979)

Seven Little Rabbits (Illustrations only, 1972)

Chanticleer and the Fox (Illustrations only, 1958)

King of Wreck Island (1941)

Åke and His World (Illustrations only, 1940)

Cooney's Major Literary Awards

1989 Boston Globe–Horn Book Picture Book Honor Book
   Island Boy

1983 American Book Award
   Miss Rumphius

1980 Caldecott Medal
   Ox-Cart Man

1959 Caldecott Medal
   Chanticleer and the Fox

their friends. Because Cooney wrote and illustrated folktales, nursery rhymes, and myths from around the world, she traveled extensively to do her research. She wanted to make sure everything—the landscapes, the buildings, the people, and even the light in the air and the color of the sky—was exactly right.

When an editor asked, "How would you like to illustrate a Mother Goose in French?" Cooney didn't hesitate. Packing up her children, she set off for France the following summer. France, Spain, Switzerland, Ireland, England, Haiti, India, Tunisia, Greece—no country was too far away if Cooney needed to research a book. And she was just as careful about her writing as she was about her drawing.

Of all her many books, Barbara Cooney said four were closest to her heart—*Miss Rumphius, Island Boy: Story and Pictures, Hattie and the Wild Waves: A Story from Brooklyn,* and *Eleanor.* These are jewels—but so are the many, many other books she left for readers to treasure.

> " '. . . A man's reach should exceed his grasp.' So should a child's. For myself, I will never talk down to—or draw down to—children."

❧

WHERE TO FIND OUT MORE ABOUT BARBARA COONEY

BOOKS

McElmeel, Sharron L. *100 Most Popular Picture Book Authors and Illustrators: Biographical Sketches and Bibliographies.* Englewood, Colo.: Libraries Unlimited, 2000.

Rockman, Connie C., ed. *The Ninth Book of Junior Authors and Illustrators.* New York: H. W. Wilson Company, 2004.

WEB SITES

CAROL HURST'S CHILDREN'S LITERATURE SITE
http://www.carolhurst.com/newsletters/32dnewsletters.html
To read a biographical sketch of Barbara Cooney and descriptions of her famous books

DENISE ORTAKALES
http://www.ortakales.com/illustrators/Cooney.html
For biographical information and links

———

COONEY'S ART HAS OFTEN BEEN DESCRIBED AS PRIMITIVE OR FOLK ART. THIS ART STYLE WENT WELL WITH THE KIND OF STORIES SHE USUALLY CHOSE TO WRITE AND ILLUSTRATE—FOLKTALES, NURSERY RHYMES, MYTHS, LEGENDS, AND HISTORICAL BIOGRAPHIES.

Floyd Cooper

Born: January 8, 1956

His warm artwork, often in earth tones of gold and brown, make Floyd Cooper's books special. His illustration technique is called oil wash. In this process, Cooper covers an illustration board with paint and then creates images by erasing them out of the paint.

Floyd Cooper was born on January 8, 1956, in Tulsa, Oklahoma. He lived there in tenement housing with his family. They didn't have much money, but Floyd's mother inspired her children to be creative and to make something of themselves. Cooper remembers that

FLOYD COOPER FIRST REMEMBERS DRAWING WHEN HE WAS JUST THREE YEARS OLD. HE PICKED UP A PIECE OF SHEETROCK AT THE SITE OF A HOUSE HIS FATHER WAS BUILDING AND STARTED SCRATCHING OUT A PICTURE.

as a young boy he was always drawing something.

After earning a bachelor of fine arts degree from the University of Oklahoma, Cooper worked in advertising. Then he moved to New York City, hoping to become a famous illustrator. When that didn't work out, he began creating artwork for children's books. And he has never regretted that turn of events!

The first book he illustrated was *Grandpa's Face*, written

> *"I feel children's books play a role in counteracting all the violence and other negative images conveyed in the media."*

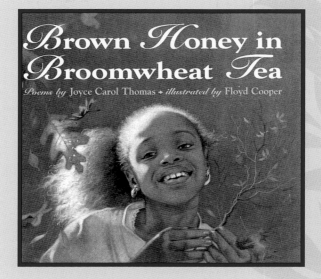

A Selected Bibliography of Cooper's Work

Most Precious Gift: A Story of the Nativity (Illustrations only, 2006)
Jump! From the Life of Michael Jordan (2004)
Mississippi Morning (Illustrations only, 2004)
Danitra Brown Leaves Town (Illustrations only, 2002)
Freedom School, Yes! (Illustrations only, 2001)
A Child Is Born (Illustrations only, 2000)
Sweet, Sweet Memory (Illustrations only, 2000)
Granddaddy's Street Songs (Illustrations only, 1999)
Cumbayah (1998)
I Have Heard of a Land (Illustrations only, 1998)
Ma Dear's Aprons (Illustrations only, 1997)
Miz Berlin Walks (Illustrations only, 1997)
Mandela: From the Life of the South African Statesman (1996)
One April Morning: Children Remember the Oklahoma City Bombing (Illustrations only, 1996)
Satchmo's Blues (Illustrations only, 1996)
Coming Home: From the Life of Langston Hughes (1994)
Meet Danitra Brown (Illustrations only, 1994)
Brown Honey in Broomwheat Tea: Poems (Illustrations only, 1993)
Reflections of a Black Cowboy (Illustrations only, 1991)
Grandpa's Face (Illustrations only, 1988)

Cooper's Major Literary Awards

1999 Coretta Scott King Illustrator Honor Book
  I Have Heard of a Land

1995 Coretta Scott King Illustrator Honor Book
  Meet Danitra Brown

1994 Coretta Scott King Illustrator Honor Book
  Brown Honey in Broomwheat Tea: Poems

by Eloise Greenfield. Both critics and readers loved his work, so his career as a children's illustrator flourished quickly.

Over the years, Cooper has illustrated many books about African American culture. His oil creations invite readers to learn about neighborhoods and family relationships, as well as about the lives of famous leaders, writers, and musicians.

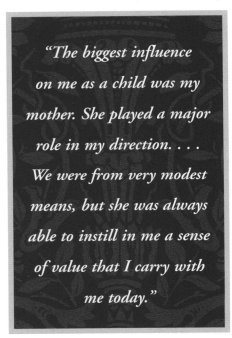

"*The biggest influence on me as a child was my mother. She played a major role in my direction. . . . We were from very modest means, but she was always able to instill in me a sense of value that I carry with me today.*"

Floyd Cooper has written some of the books he illustrated. One example is *Coming Home: From the Life of Langston Hughes,* a biography of the famous African American poet. He has written and illustrated *Mandela: From the Life of the South African Statesman,* a biography of this courageous South African leader. He has also illustrated *Cumbayah,* a look at a song that people of all ages love to sing around campfires.

One of Cooper's favorite projects was illustrating *Satchmo's Blues,* a book written by Alan Schroeder about jazz musician Louis Armstrong. He has also illustrated collections of poems, a book about Japanese

IN ADDITION TO MAKING A LIVING IN ADVERTISING, COOPER WORKED FOR A TIME AS A GREETING-CARD DESIGNER FOR HALLMARK.

culture, and *One April Morning: Children Remember the Oklahoma City Bombing,* a book about the 1995 attack on a federal office building.

Floyd Cooper lives with his wife and children in New Jersey. He enjoys speaking with young readers and talking about his art.

❧

WHERE TO FIND OUT MORE ABOUT FLOYD COOPER

BOOKS

Children's Literature Review, Vol. 60. Detroit: Gale, 2000.

Cullinam, Bernice E. and Diane G. Person. *Continuum Encyclopedia of Children's Literature.* New York: Coninuum International, 2001.

McElmeel, Sharron L. *100 Most Popular Picture Book Authors and Illustrators: Biographical Sketches and Bibliographies.* Englewood, Colo.: Libraries Unlimited, 2000.

WEB SITES

HOUGHTON MIFFLIN: MEET THE AUTHOR/ILLUSTRATOR
http://www.eduplace.com/kids/hmr/mtai/fcooper.html
To read a biographical sketch and booklist for Floyd Cooper

KIDS POINT
http://www.kidspoint.org/columns2.asp?column_id=1125&column_type=author
For biographical information and links to other sites

COOPER IS A FAN OF ALL KINDS OF MUSIC, INCLUDING JAZZ AND THE BLUES, BUT HE SAYS HE HAS "TWO LEFT EARS."

Susan Cooper

Born: May 23, 1935

When Susan Cooper was ten years old, she wrote three puppet plays (the puppeteer was the boy next door). She also wrote a weekly newspaper with her piano teacher's son. And she wrote, illustrated, and sewed together her first book. "My uncle found it in a drawer and came and told me that he liked it, and I was so appalled that somebody had read it that I burst into tears and tore it up," she says.

Susan Cooper was born in Buckinghamshire, England, on May 23, 1935. History was all around her. From her bedroom window, she could see Windsor Castle. An Iron Age fort and part of a road built by the Romans long ago were not far from her home.

Cooper attended Oxford University and was the first woman to edit the university's student newspaper. After graduating, she worked for the *Sunday Times* in London.

In her spare time, she wrote a science fiction novel for adults, *Mandrake,* published in 1964. She heard about a contest for a children's

WHEN SUSAN COOPER WENT TO WORK FOR THE *SUNDAY TIMES* NEWSPAPER, HER BOSS WAS IAN FLEMING, THE CREATOR OF THE FICTIONAL SECRET AGENT JAMES BOND.

book and wrote *Over Sea, Under Stone*. It started as a simple adventure—until she found herself creating Merriman Lyon, a mysterious character who turns out to be Merlin, the wizard of the legends of King Arthur.

Over Sea, Under Stone is the first of the Dark Is Rising series—five stories filled with adventure, a battle between good and evil, and characters based on Arthurian legend. At that

> *"Read, read, read, anything and everything, prose and poetry and drama. Preferably good stuff, so that its rhythms will echo through your head ever afterwards, even when you aren't aware of them."*

time, however, Cooper had no idea that she had started a series. It was eight years before the second book was published. In the meantime, Cooper fell in love with a professor at Massachusetts Institute of Technology and moved to the United States to marry him. She raised his three children and had two of her own. She also wrote articles for a British newspaper, and wrote a novel, *Dawn of Fear,* about a child who lives through the bombing of London in World War II (1939–1945), as Cooper had.

In time, Cooper became homesick for England. One day, while skiing, she had an idea: She would write four interlocking books about the characters and situations she had created for *Over Sea, Under Stone*—four books about England. Over the next few years, she wrote *The Dark Is Rising, Greenwitch, The Grey King,* and *Silver on the Tree.*

COOPER'S BEST-KNOWN WORK FOR ADULTS ISN'T A BOOK BUT A PLAY, *FOXFIRE*, WHICH RAN FOR SEVEN MONTHS ON BROADWAY. HER COAUTHOR, AND THE STAR OF THE PLAY, WAS ACTOR HUME CRONYN, TO WHOM SHE IS NOW MARRIED.

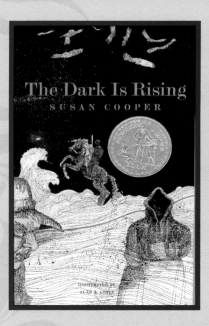

A Selected Bibliography of Cooper's Work

Sea Change (2006)

Magician's Boy (2005)

To Be a Pilgrim (2004)

Frog (2002)

King of Shadows (1999)

The Boggart and the Monster (1997)

Danny and the Kings (1993)

The Boggart (1993)

Tam Lin (1991)

The Selkie Girl (1986)

The Silver Cow: A Welsh Tale (1983)

Jethro and the Jumbie (1979)

Silver on the Tree (1977)

The Grey King (1975)

Greenwitch (1974)

The Dark Is Rising (1973)

Dawn of Fear (1970)

Over Sea, Under Stone (1965)

Cooper's Major Literary Awards

2000 Boston Globe–Horn Book Fiction Honor Book
  King of Shadows

1976 Newbery Medal
  The Grey King

1974 Newbery Honor Book

1973 Boston Globe–Horn Book Fiction Award
  The Dark Is Rising

The stories were set in the towns and villages she knew as a child and described legendary figures such as Merlin and King Arthur, as well as invented characters, such as Bran, Arthur's son.

Then Susan Cooper turned to other projects. She wrote stories for younger readers, including *The Selkie Girl.* She wrote about the humorous side of legend in her books about the Boggart, a mischievous spirit who lives in a Scottish castle. She also wrote television movies and several plays. It wasn't until 1999 that she returned to the young-adult audience, with *King of Shadows,* the story of a boy actor in 1999 who is transported to 1599, where he gets

to work with William
Shakespeare.

In 1996, Cooper
married actor Hume
Cronyn, who died in 2003.
Susan Cooper lives in
Connecticut.

"At the back of every writer's head there's a small locked room, where the imagination lives. The room has a door with no handle; you can't open it. But once in a great while, for no apparent reason, the door swings open and an idea pops out."

WHERE TO FIND OUT MORE ABOUT SUSAN COOPER

BOOKS

Rockman, Connie C., ed. *Eighth Book of Junior Authors and Illustrators.*
New York: H. W. Wilson Company, 2000.

Silvey, Anita, ed. *The Essential Guide to Children's Books and Their Creators.*
Boston: Houghton Mifflin Company, 2002.

Sutherland, Zena. *Children & Books.* 9th ed. New York: Addison Wesley Longman, 1997.

WEB SITES

THE AUTHOR: SUSAN COOPER
http://hosted.ukoln.ac.uk/stories/stories/cooper/interview.htm
To read an interview with Susan Cooper

KIDSREADS.COM
http://www.kidsreads.com/authors/au-cooper-susan.asp
To read an autobiographical sketch by Susan Cooper

WHEN SUSAN COOPER FIRST WROTE *OVER SEA, UNDER STONE,* TWENTY
PUBLISHERS REJECTED THE STORY.

Lucy Cousins

Born: February 10, 1964

Early in her career, writer and illustrator Lucy Cousins brought some of her work to Wendy Boase, a children's book editor. "I had never seen anything so original," says Boase. "There was nothing quite like her work." Cousins uses thick lines and bold colors to make very simple pictures. Her most famous character is Maisy the mouse. In 1990, the first Maisy book was published. The bright little mouse was an instant hit with tiny children. Babies and toddlers also love lifting the flaps and pulling the tabs in many of Cousins's books.

Today, Maisy is one of the most popular characters among

MAISY'S HEAD IS NEVER SHOWN FROM THE FRONT. IT IS ALWAYS SEEN IN A SIDE VIEW, EVEN ON TELEVISION SHOWS.

very young children. More than 9 million Maisy books have been sold. They have been translated into twenty-one languages. Maisy even has her own television show.

Lucy Cousins was born in Reading, England, on February 10, 1964. She attended Canterbury Art College and Brighton Polytechnic. She then studied graphic design at the Royal College of Art.

Cousins had always loved the art in children's books. She would often go to bookstores to browse through the children's books. Finally, she decided to try making one herself. For her art-school graduation project, she made *Portly's Hat,* a book about a penguin.

A Selected Bibliography of Cousins's Work

Maisy, Charley, and the Wobbly Tooth (2006)
Hooray for Fish (2005)
Maisy Goes Camping (2004)
Go, Maisy, Go! (2003)
Maisy's Rainbow Dream (2003)
Jazzy in the Jungle (2002)
Doctor Maisy (2001)
Maisy's Favorite Animals (2001)
Maisy Drives the Bus (2000)
Maisy Dresses Up (1999)
Happy Birthday, Maisy (1998)
Count with Maisy (1997)
Za-Za's Baby Brother (1995)
Noah's Ark (1993)
The Little Dog Laughed (Illustrations only, 1990)
Maisy Goes Swimming (1990)
Maisy Goes to Bed (1990)
Portly's Hat (1989)

Then she heard about a competition for art students run by Macmillan, a publishing company in England. *Portly's Hat* won second prize! Macmillan soon published the book. The experience gave Cousins the confidence to try to sell more ideas to book publishers.

> *"I draw by heart. I think of what children would like by going back to my own childlike instincts."*

Since then, Lucy Cousins has turned out dozens of bright, simple books for small children. Some are about animals. Others are collections of nursery rhymes. Many are about Maisy. Maisy stories are the stuff of everyday life. She goes to bed. She goes to school. She makes gingerbread.

Maisy the mouse also stars in an award-winning television show. Cousins was very worried about what would happen to her characters and stories when they were turned into cartoons, so she is very involved in the production of the show. She can reject anything she doesn't like.

To date, Maisy has appeared in more than one hundred books and

> *"I get more pleasure and inspiration from walking around a primary school than from any art gallery."*

television shows. But Cousins is not worried about running out of ideas anytime soon. "When you live with small children, you realize there are so many little events that can be made into a story—brushing teeth, losing something, going shopping," explains Cousins. So Maisy

MAISY PRODUCTS ARE POPULAR ALL OVER THE WORLD. IN JAPAN ALONE, MORE THAN 300 MAISY PRODUCTS ARE SOLD, INCLUDING BICYCLES, STAPLERS, AND CHOPSTICKS.

and her friends will be around to entertain babies and toddlers for a long time to come.

These days, Lucy Cousins lives in Hampshire, England, with her four young children. They help her test her books. When she made her first cloth books, her daughter Josie was seven months old. "Josie looked at them and chewed on them and did all the right things," Cousins recalls. She knew she was on the right track.

❧

WHERE TO FIND OUT MORE ABOUT LUCY COUSINS

BOOKS

Rockman, Connie C., ed. *Eighth Book of Junior Authors and Illustrators.*
New York: H. W. Wilson Company, 2000.

Silvey, Anita, ed. *Children's Books and Their Creators.*
Boston: Houghton Mifflin, 1995.

WEB SITES

MAISY AT NICKJR.COM
www.nickjr.com/kids/html_site/maisy/
To find out more about Maisy's friends

WALKER BOOKS: LUCY COUSINS
http://www.walkerbooks.co.uk/Lucy-Cousins
To read about Lucy Cousins's childhood, her life as a writer and artist, and to explore her books

———

ALTHOUGH MAISY IS AN OUTGOING LITTLE MOUSE, HER CREATOR DOESN'T MUCH LIKE ATTENTION. LUCY COUSINS ALMOST NEVER DOES INTERVIEWS OR BOOK SIGNINGS.

Helen Craig

Born: August 30, 1934

Most people are in their twenties when they discover what they want to do in life," Helen Craig explains. It took her almost forty years to decide that she wanted to illustrate children's books! Since then, Craig has written and illustrated the popular *The Mouse House ABC, Susie and Alfred in The Night of the Paper Bag Monsters,* and *The Town Mouse and the Country Mouse.* She is best known as the illustrator of the Angelina Ballerina series written by Katharine Holabird.

Helen Craig was born on August 30, 1934, in London, England. She grew up in a family of artists. Her grandfather was a stage designer for the theater. Her father was an art director for films, and

---

HELEN CRAIG HAS WORKED AS A POTTER, A SCULPTOR, AND A RESTORER OF CHINESE WALLPAPER.

her brother was an illustrator and graphic designer.

"It had always been my ambition that one day I would be a creative artist of some sort," says Craig. But as a teenager, Helen did not think her art was as good as that of other members of

> *"As a child I had been strongly impressed by the books I looked at and read, and can still recall those feelings and try to remember them when working."*

her family. So instead of becoming an artist, she went to work with a photographer. She learned how to take pictures and she became a very talented photographer. Several years later, she started her own photography studio.

Craig was hired to take pictures for magazines and advertising. While she was working as a photographer, she continued to draw. She found drawing to be relaxing. She did not show her drawings to anyone, though. She was not sure her work was any good!

Craig's interest in illustrating children's books developed after her son was born in 1965. As she read books to her son, she imagined how exciting it would be to illustrate a book for children herself.

A few years later, Craig showed some of her drawings and a story she had written to an editor. The work was not published, but she was asked

---

THREE OF CRAIG'S BOOKS HAVE BEEN CHOSEN FOR THE BRITISH
BOOK DESIGN AND PRODUCTION EXHIBITIONS.

A Selected Bibliography of Craig's Work

A Very Special Secret (Illustrations only, 2006)

Angelina and Alice (Illustrations only, 2006)

Angelina Love (Illustrations only, 2005)

Angelina and the Princess (Illustrations only, 2004)

Angelina and the Butterfly (Illustrations only, 2002)

Rosy's Visitors (Illustrations only, 2002)

Angelina's Birthday (Illustrations only, 2001)

Angelina's Halloween (Illustrations only, 2000)

Panda's New Toy (Illustrations only, 1999)

Turnover Tuesday (Illustrations only, 1998)

Charlie and Tyler at the Seashore (1995)

Susie and Alfred in The Night of the Paper Bag Monsters (1994)

I See the Moon and the Moon Sees Me: Helen Craig's Book of Nursery Rhymes (1992)

The Town Mouse and the Country Mouse (1992)

Susie and Alfred in The Knight, the Princess and the Dragon (1987)

Susie and Alfred in A Welcome for Annie (1986)

Angelina Ballerina (Illustrations only, 1983)

The Mouse House ABC (1979)

Wishing Gold (Illustrations only, 1970)

to illustrate a book written by another author. That book, written by Robert Nye, was called *Wishing Gold*. It was published in 1970. Craig went on to illustrate other books written by other authors. *The Mouse House ABC* was the first book she wrote and illustrated. It was published in 1979.

The inspiration for Craig's illustrations comes from a

"Every illustrator always wants to produce beautiful pictures, but for me the most important element is to make the characters communicate with each other. I hope I manage to do this."

variety of places. She uses memories from her childhood to create many of her illustrations. "Now that I'm an illustrator myself, I try to make my pictures live for the children who look at them, as those pictures did for me when I was a child," Craig notes.

Helen Craig continues to write and illustrate books for children. She lives in Aylesbury, England.

❧

WHERE TO FIND OUT MORE ABOUT HELEN CRAIG

BOOKS

Rockman, Connie C., ed. *Eighth Book of Junior Authors and Illustrators.* New York: H. W. Wilson Company, 2000.

Silvey, Anita, ed. *The Essential Guide to Children's Books and Their Creators.* Boston: Houghton Mifflin, 2002.

WEB SITES

ANGELINA BALLERINA
http://www.angelinaballerina.com/
To play a ballerina game and make mini-posters

TOONHOUND—ANGELINA BALLERINA
http://www.toonhound.com/angelina.htm
To read an episode list of the television series

HELEN CRAIG DESIGNED AN ANGELINA BALLERINA DOLL THAT WAS BASED ON HER DRAWINGS FOR THE BOOKS.

Sharon Creech

Born: July 29, 1945

In *Walk Two Moons*, thirteen-year-old Salamanca Tree Hiddle searches for her mother, while *The Wanderer,* Sophie, also thirteen, learns about her family on a sailing trip across the ocean. Mary Lou Finney tells about her thirteenth summer in *Absolutely Normal Chaos.*

With these teenage characters, Sharon Creech writes stories of love and loss, happiness and heartache.

Sharon Creech was born on July 29, 1945, in South Euclid, Ohio, a suburb of Cleveland. She grew up in a large family, in a house full of people who loved to tell stories. As a young woman, Sharon was always drawn to reading and writing, and she collected paper, pens, and books. After high school, she enrolled at Hiram College

SHARON CREECH WROTE TWO BOOKS UNDER THE NAME SHARON RIGG—
THE RECITAL AND *NICKEL MALLEY.* THEY WERE PUBLISHED ONLY IN ENGLAND.

in Ohio, where she earned her bachelor's degree. Then she moved on to George Mason University in Virginia, where she earned her master's degree.

Creech's first jobs after college were working as a researcher for the Federal Theater Project Archives and as an editorial assistant at *Congressional Quarterly*, in Washington, D.C. She found these positions to be terribly boring, though, because they involved facts and

"I don't remember the titles of books I read as a child, but I do remember the experience of reading—of drifting into the pages and living in someone else's world."

A Selected Bibliography of Creech's Work

Who's That Baby? New Baby Songs (2005)
Replay: A New Book (2005)
Granny Torrelli Makes Soup (2003)
Ruby Holler (2002)
A Fine, Fine School (2001)
Love That Dog (2001)
Fishing in the Air (2000)
The Wanderer (2000)
Bloomability (1998)
Chasing Redbird (1997)
Pleasing the Ghost (1996)
Absolutely Normal Chaos (1995)
Walk Two Moons (1994)

Creech's Major Literary Awards

2003 Carnegie Medal
    Ruby Holler

2001 Newbery Honor Book
    The Wanderer

1995 Newbery Medal
    Walk Two Moons

> *"I wanted to be many things when I grew up: a painter, an ice skater, a singer, a teacher, and a reporter. . . . I soon learned that I would make a terrible reporter because when I didn't like the facts, I changed them."*

numbers rather than thoughts and ideas. In Washington, Creech got married, had two children, and then divorced.

Creech's next move was more exciting. She and her children left the United States and moved to England, where she taught literature at a boarding school. There she met Lyle Rigg, an assistant headmaster, and they were married. They remained in England for a time. Next they were transferred to a boarding school in Switzerland but later returned to England.

Through these adventures, Sharon Creech realized she had much to write about. She published her first book for young readers, *Absolutely Normal Chaos*, in England in 1990, but it was not released in the United States until five years later. In the meantime, she wrote *Walk Two Moons*, the book that made her famous as an author.

Her stories about young people appeal to readers because they deal with real problems in a real way. Creech's characters worry about families and schoolwork as well as about boyfriends and girlfriends. Creech also

---

THE TITLE FOR *WALK TWO MOONS* CAME FROM THIS MESSAGE IN A FORTUNE COOKIE: "DON'T JUDGE A MAN UNTIL YOU'VE WALKED TWO MOONS IN HIS MOCCASINS."

sets her stories in places all over the world—in cities and towns she has lived in and visited.

As much as she enjoyed her time in Europe, Sharon Creech missed the United States. So she and her husband recently moved to New Jersey. She continues to write, and Rigg is the headmaster of a private school. When Creech is not writing, she still enjoys teaching and tutoring, and she loves spending time outdoors and with her grown children.

∿

WHERE TO FIND OUT MORE ABOUT SHARON CREECH

BOOKS

Beacham's Guide to Literature for Young Adults, Vol. 12. Detroit: Gale, 2001.

McElmeel, Sharron L. *Children's Authors and Illustrators Too Good to Miss: Biographical Sketches and Bibliographies.* Englewood, Colo: Libraries Unlimited, 2004.

Silvey, Anita, ed. *The Essential Guide to Children's Books and Their Creators.* Boston: Houghton Mifflin Company, 2002.

WEB SITES

EDUCATIONAL PAPERBACK ASSOCIATION
http://edupaperback.org/showauth.cfm?authid=51
To read an autobiographical sketch by and booklist for Sharon Creech

SHARON CREECH HOME PAGE
http://sharoncreech.com/
To read a brief biography about Sharon Creech and learn more about her books

———

IN ADDITION TO HER BOOKS, CREECH WROTE THE PLAY *THE CENTER OF THE UNIVERSE: WAITING FOR THE GIRL*, WHICH WAS PRODUCED IN NEW YORK CITY IN 1992.

Donald Crews

Born: August 30, 1938

The things that catch Donald Crews's eye are a lot like the things that catch the attention of children. He is interested in dots, motion, and shapes. As an artist, he has a fresh way of looking at the world. Through his bold, solid illustrations, simple things such as a steam train chugging along the tracks come alive.

Donald Crews was born on August 30, 1938, in Newark, New Jersey, in a large African American family. Donald's father was a railroad trackman, responsible for the stretches of rails that carried the swift-moving steam trains that fascinated his son. His mother was a dressmaker and craftswoman.

DONALD CREWS'S CREATIVE USE OF PHOTOGRAPHS TO ILLUSTRATE CHILDREN'S BOOKS HAS GAINED HIM MUCH PRAISE. IN *CAROUSEL*, FOR EXAMPLE, HE USED A COLLAGE OF PICTURES OF A CAROUSEL TO CREATE THE IMPRESSION OF ITS CIRCULAR MOVEMENT.

Crews attributes his artistic interests to his mother. Her dressmaking tools resembled the tools of the graphic artist. She worked with geometric patterns and chose swaths of cloth for their colors and textures. Donald's brother and two sisters all inherited this creative impulse.

For as long as he can remember, Crews has been sketching. His skill in the visual arts won him a place at an arts high school, where he devoted most of his time to painting, drawing, and photography. After high school, he attended the Cooper Union for the Advancement of Science and Art in New York City.

At Cooper Union, Crews met a fellow student—author, artist, and designer Ann Jonas. After working as an assistant art director at *Dance* magazine and a staff designer for a studio in New York City, Crews joined the U.S. Army. He married Ann in 1964, while stationed in Germany. They had two daughters, Nina Melissa and Amy Marshanna.

In Germany, Crews wrote and illustrated his first children's book—*We Read: A to Z.* In this book, vivid illustrations introduce the letters of the alphabet. Crews originally planned to include

"I take photographs . . . more than I sketch things. If I need information, I'd just as soon photograph it . . . and use that for inspiration."

CREWS'S ABILITY TO EXPRESS AN IDEA CLEARLY IN IMAGES LED HIM TO ILLUSTRATE A SERIES OF MATH AND SCIENCE BOOKS, INCLUDING *FRACTIONS ARE PARTS OF THINGS* AND *ABC OF ECOLOGY.*

A Selected Bibliography of Crews's Work

How Many Birds Flew Away? A Counting Book with a Difference (2005)

Cloudy Day/Sunny Day (1999)

Night at the Fair (1997)

More Than One (Illustrations only, 1996)

Sail Away (1995)

Tomorrow's Alphabet (Illustrations only, 1995)

When This Box Is Full (Illustrations only, 1993)

Each Orange Had Eight Slices: A Counting Book (Illustrations only, 1992)

Shortcut (1992)

Bigmama's (1991)

Flying (1986)

Bicycle Race (1985)

School Bus (1984)

Parade (1983)

Carousel (1982)

Harbor (1982)

Light (1981)

Truck (1980)

Blue Sea (Illustrations only, 1979)

Freight Train (1978)

Rain (Illustrations only, 1978)

Eclipse: Darkness in Daytime (Illustrations only, 1973)

ABC of Ecology (Illustrations only, 1972)

Fractions Are Parts of Things (Illustrations only, 1971)

ABC Science Experiments (Illustrations only, 1970)

Ten Black Dots (1968)

We Read: A to Z (1967)

Crews's Major Literary Awards

1981 Caldecott Honor Book
  Truck

1979 Caldecott Honor Book
  Freight Train

the project in his portfolio, but in 1967, *We Read: A to Z* was accepted for publication. Crews's powerful pictures hold the very young reader's attention and are ideally suited for those trying to grasp reading basics. The next year, Crews's *Ten Black Dots,* which introduces numbers, was published.

The memory of sitting on his grandparents' porch in Cottondale, Florida, and watching the trains go by, inspired Crews's 1978 award-winning *Freight Train.* The experience

> *"It's very heady to be called an author and writer, to know that things you create could be useful."*

convinced the author/illustrator that he could create picture books for a living, and so he left his career as a designer.

Today, Donald Crews lives with his wife in New York. As a full-time writer, Crews travels to schools and meets the children, parents, and teachers who read his books in the classroom and at home. He is always surprised by their enthusiasm, which convinces him anew that his job is, after all, important work.

❧

WHERE TO FIND OUT MORE ABOUT DONALD CREWS

BOOKS

McElmeel, Sharron L. *100 Most Popular Picture Book Authors and Illustrators: Biographical Sketches and Bibliographies.* Englewood, Colo.: Libraries Unlimited, 2000.

Silvey, Anita, ed. *The Essential Guide to Children's Books and Their Creators.* Boston: Houghton Mifflin Company, 2002.

WEB SITES

HARPER CHILDRENS
http://www.harperchildrens.com/catalog/author_xml.asp?authorid=16149
To read a biographical sketch of the author and a list of works

HORN BOOK—DONALD CREWS
http://www.hbook.com/studio_crews.shtml
To read an excerpt from the *Horn Book* about why Crews likes to draw with pencils

NATIONAL CENTER FOR CHILDREN'S ILLUSTRATED LITERATURE: DONALD CREWS
http://www.nccil.org/dcrews.html
To read about Donald Crews's life and work

IN 1979 CREWS'S *FREIGHT TRAIN* WAS EXHIBITED IN THE AMERICAN INSTITUTE OF GRAPHIC ARTS CHILDREN'S BOOK SHOW.

Christopher Paul Curtis

Born: May 10, 1954

C hristopher Paul Curtis was not sure he could be a successful writer. "I give a lot of the credit for my writing career to my wife," Curtis notes. "She had more faith in my ability to write than I did." His first book was published in 1995. *The Watsons Go to Birmingham— 1963* is a novel about an African American family who travel South for

a vacation during the civil rights era. In 1999, Curtis published his next book, *Bud, Not Buddy,* about a motherless boy who takes to the road in 1936.

Christopher Paul Curtis was born on May 10, 1954, in Flint, Michigan. He grew up and went to school there. His parents had strict rules that Christopher was expected to obey. When he finished high school, he wanted to go to college, but he had to get a job and earn money instead.

CURTIS STUDIED POLITICAL SCIENCE IN COLLEGE AND HELPED RUN THE CAMPAIGN FOR A U.S. CONGRESSIONAL CANDIDATE.

Christopher's father worked at an automotive-assembly plant in Flint. Curtis took a job fitting doors on the cars at the plant. He held that job for more than thirteen years, working on his writing when he could.

After several years, Curtis began attending the University of Michigan at night. As a student, he won a prize for his writing. His wife encouraged him to pursue a career as a writer. They decided that he would quit his job at the plant to concentrate on his writing. He completed his college degree in 1996.

> *"I often tell students that the best practice for writing is to do it at every opportunity."*

A Selected Bibliography of Curtis's Work

Mr. Chickee's Funny Money (2005)
Bucking the Sarge (2004)
Bud, Not Buddy (1999)
The Watsons Go to Birmingham—1963 (1995)

Curtis's Major Literary Awards

2000 Coretta Scott King Author Award
2000 Newbery Medal
  Bud, Not Buddy

1996 Coretta Scott King Author Honor Book
1996 Newbery Honor Book
  The Watsons Go to Birmingham—1963

> *"I used to write during breaks because it took me away from being in the factory. I didn't like being there so I would sit down and write. It was much like reading, it would take me away from where I was."*

Every day Curtis worked at a table in the children's section of the local library. He wrote on sheets of paper. His son took his father's words and typed them into a computer. When the book was finished, Curtis entered it into a national writing contest. Although the book did not win the contest, an editor of a publishing company liked the manuscript enough to publish it! *The Watsons Go to Birmingham—1963* went on to win several awards.

Curtis has a strong connection to the city where he grew up. All his books are set in Flint. He has many memories from growing up there and uses the city's history in his books. Another important influence in his writing was his job at the automobile plant. "My job was hanging doors, and I still have nightmares about the numbing repetitiveness of the work, but I believe it helped me become a writer," he explains. "It helped me develop the discipline to write daily."

Curtis now lives with his family in Windsor, Ontario, Canada. He continues to write books for young adults. He also travels and visits

---

ACTOR WHOOPI GOLDBERG PURCHASED THE RIGHTS TO ADAPT *THE WATSONS GO TO BIRMINGHAM—1963* INTO A MOTION PICTURE.

schools to talk to young people about his writing. "Many times young people feel that writing is, or should be, the result of a consultation with some mysterious, hard-to-find muse," says Curtis. "I don't think so. I think in many ways writing is much like learning a second language or playing a sport or mastering a musical instrument: the more you do it, the better you become at it."

❧

WHERE TO FIND OUT MORE ABOUT CHRISTOPHER PAUL CURTIS

BOOKS

McElmeel, Sharron L. *Children's Authors and Illustrators Too Good to Miss: Biographical Sketches and Bibliographies.* Englewood, Colo: Libraries Unlimited, 2004.

Rockman, Connie C., ed. *Eighth Book of Junior Authors and Illustrators.* New York: H. W. Wilson Company, 2000.

Silvey, Anita, ed. *The Essential Guide to Children's Books and Their Creators.* Boston: Houghton Mifflin Company, 2002.

Thrash Murphy, Barbara. *Black Authors and Illustrators of Books for Children and Young Adults: A Biographical Dictionary, 3rd edition.* New York: Garland, 1999.

WEB SITES

EDUCATIONAL PAPERBACK ASSOCIATION
http://edupaperback.org/showauth.cfm?authid=52
To read an autobiographical sketch of Christopher Paul Curtis

RANDOM HOUSE
http://www.randomhouse.com/features/christopherpaulcurtis/
To read a biographical sketch of the author

BOTH OF CURTIS'S GRANDFATHERS HAD INTERESTING JOBS. ONE OF HIS GRANDFATHERS WAS A PITCHER IN THE NEGRO BASEBALL LEAGUE AND THE OTHER WAS THE LEADER OF A BAND.

Karen Cushman

Born: October 4, 1941

Karen Cushman was fifty-three years old when she published her first book. It wasn't that she hadn't been interested in writing before that, however. Cushman spent much of her childhood reading her way through the town library and writing stories, plays, poems, and new plots for Elvis Presley movies. But growing up in a working-class neighborhood in the 1940s, she didn't realize that she could make a career out of writing.

She was born Karen Lipski in Chicago on October 4, 1941. Her family moved to Tarzana, California, when she was eleven. Karen did well in school and won a scholarship to any college of her choice. She chose Stanford University, where she studied English and Greek, thinking she might become an archaeologist. Instead, she got a job working for the phone company, the first of a series of boring jobs. She quit them all.

CUSHMAN'S WRITING AS A TEENAGER INCLUDED "JINGLE BAGELS," A CHRISTMAS/HANUKKAH PLAY IN WHICH SANTA CLAUS GOES DOWN THE WRONG CHIMNEY.

She met her husband, Philip Cushman, when he was studying to be a rabbi. They moved to Oregon, where, Karen says, "I wove and made black-berry jam and had a daughter, Leah." Her daughter was born in 1973.

After a few years, the Cushmans moved back to California. Karen got a master's degree in counseling and another in museum studies—a subject she taught for many years thereafter.

"I like writing because it's something I can do at home barefoot; because I can lie on my bed and read and call it work; because I am always making up stories in my head anyway and I might as well make a living from them."

Leah grew up and grew out of the children's books she and her mother had read together, but Karen Cushman remained interested. She would tell her husband about ideas for books of her own. One day he replied, "Don't tell me about it. Write it."

So Cushman did just that. She wrote seven pages about a girl in the Middle Ages who thinks she is going to be forced to marry a rich landowner. Then came the hard part—finding out how people actually lived in the thirteenth century. She needed to know about their food and their table manners, their beliefs and their superstitions, how they cured a toothache, how they took a bath. She researched and she read.

WHEN CUSHMAN WAS WRITING HER FIRST NOVEL, MANY PEOPLE TRIED TO DISCOURAGE HER. THEY TOLD HER THAT HISTORICAL FICTION WOULDN'T SELL AND THAT BOYS WOULDN'T READ A STORY ABOUT GIRLS.

A Selected Bibliography of Cushman's Work

Loud Silence of Francine Green (2006)

Rodzina (2003)

Matilda Bone (2000)

The Ballad of Lucy Whipple (1996)

The Midwife's Apprentice (1995)

Catherine, Called Birdy (1994)

Cushman's Major Literary Awards

1996 Newbery Medal
  The Midwife's Apprentice

1995 Newbery Honor Book
  Catherine, Called Birdy

Then she wrote. Three years later, her book was finished—*Catherine, Called Birdy.* The novel was very popular and received several awards, including the Newbery Honor.

Cushman's second book was also set in the Middle Ages, so it took only six months to write. *The Midwife's Apprentice* tells the story of an "unwashed, unnourished, unloved, and unlovely" girl named Brat, who learns how to deliver babies and discovers much about herself at the same time. Published in 1995, it won the Newbery Medal.

> *"I used to imagine I was the only child ever kidnapped from gypsies and sold to regular people."*

For her third book, Cushman switched to the nineteenth century. She read that 90 percent of the people who took part in the California Gold Rush in 1849 were men. She went back to the library to do the research, and in 1996 published *The Ballad of Lucy Whipple,* the story of a twelve-year-old girl "who didn't want any part of the Gold Rush but had no choice." Another medieval book, *Matilda Bone,* set in the world of medicine, followed in 2000.

"I've always been a late bloomer," Cushman said in an interview. "But I always eventually bloom. Here I am making a new career late in life and having a wonderful time."

❧

WHERE TO FIND OUT MORE ABOUT KAREN CUSHMAN

BOOK

McElmeel, Sharron L. *Children's Authors and Illustrators Too Good to Miss: Biographical Sketches and Bibliographies.* Englewood, Colo: Libraries Unlimited, 2004.

WEB SITES

INTERNET PUBLIC LIBRARY KIDSPACE
http://www.ipl.org/div/kidspace/askauthor/cushmanbio.html
To read Karen Cushman's answers to questions submitted by children as well as FAQ about her life and work

KAREN CUSHMAN HOME PAGE
http://www.karencushman.com/
This site features biographical information and a booklist

───

WHEN *CATHERINE, CALLED BIRDY* WAS NAMED A NEWBERY HONOR BOOK, CUSHMAN WAS SO NEW TO CHILDREN'S LITERATURE THAT SHE HAD TO FIND OUT WHAT THE NEWBERY MEDAL WAS BEFORE SHE REALIZED HOW WELL SHE HAD DONE.

Roald Dahl

Born: September 13, 1916
Died: November 23, 1990

Roald Dahl never intended to be a writer. He wanted to visit faraway countries and have exciting adventures. It was almost by accident that his first story was published. After that, he wrote many books, plays, and movie screenplays for adults and children. He is best known for the children's books *James and the Giant Peach: A Children's Story; Charlie and the Chocolate Factory; The Magic Finger; Matilda;* and *Danny, the Champion of the World.*

Roald Dahl was born on September 13, 1916, in Llandaff, Wales. He had five sisters and one brother. Sadly, his father died when Roald was four years old.

Roald was an energetic child who loved getting into mischief. He attended an all-boys boarding school where discipline was very strict.

DAHL INVENTED A NEW WORD FOR HIS BOOK *THE GREMLINS.*
THE WORD WAS "GREMLIN"!

Roald was often beaten when he got into trouble. This cruelty became a part of the stories he wrote as an adult.

After high school, Roald's mother wanted him to attend Oxford University, a famous school in England. Dahl had no interest in going to Oxford. He wanted a job with a company that would send him to faraway places. Shell Oil hired Dahl and sent him to Tanzania.

In 1939, Dahl became a fighter pilot for Great Britain in World War II (1939–1945). Flying over Egypt, his plane was hit by machine-gun fire and crashed. He was badly injured and ultimately had to stop flying.

Then Dahl was transferred to Washington, D.C. There the

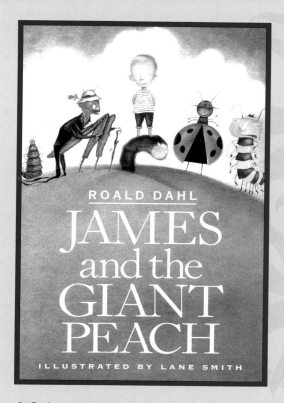

A Selected Bibliography of Dahl's Work

Matilda (1988)
Boy: Tales of Childhood (1984)
The Witches (1983)
The BFG (1982)
The Twits (1980)
The Enormous Crocodile (1978)
The Wonderful Story of Henry Sugar and Six More (1977)
Danny, the Champion of the World (1975)
Charlie and the Great Glass Elevator (1972)
Fantastic Mr. Fox (1970)
The Magic Finger (1966)
Charlie and the Chocolate Factory (1964)
James and the Giant Peach: A Children's Story (1961)
The Gremlins (1943)

Dahl's Major Literary Award

1985 Boston Globe–Horn Book Nonfiction Honor Book
  Boy: Tales of Childhood

> *"If you think a child is getting bored, you must think up something that jolts it back. Something that tickles. You have to know what children like."*

Saturday Evening Post magazine asked him to write a story about being a fighter pilot. It earned him $1,000 and was the beginning of Dahl's writing career. "But becoming a writer was pure fluke," remembered Dahl. "Without being asked to, I doubt if I'd ever have thought of it."

Dahl wrote his first children's story, *The Gremlins,* in 1943. It was a success, and Dahl became a full-time writer. During the next seventeen years, he wrote many short stories for adults. During this time, he married actor Patricia O'Neal. They had one son and four daughters (one of whom died in childhood).

At home, Roald Dahl began making up stories for his children at bedtime. Soon, he was writing these stories for publication. In 1961, he published a children's book about the adventures of a young orphan who is forced to live with his two wicked aunts. It was called *James and the Giant Peach: A Children's Story.*

From that time on, Dahl focused on writing for children. The cruelty he remembered from his own childhood was a common theme in his stories. His stories were often fantasies and adventures told with humor and

DAHL WROTE MOST OF HIS CHILDREN'S BOOKS IN A TINY HUT IN AN ORCHARD AT HIS HOME IN BUCKINGHAMSHIRE, ENGLAND.

understanding. Over the years, Dahl's books have sold millions of copies.

After Dahl and O'Neal divorced in 1983, Dahl remarried. Roald Dahl continued writing until his death on November 23, 1990, in Oxford, England. He was seventy-four.

> *"The writer for children must be a jokey sort of a fellow. He must like simple tricks and jokes and riddles and other childish things."*

WHERE TO FIND OUT MORE ABOUT ROALD DAHL

BOOKS

Dahl, Roald. *Going Solo.* New York: Puffin Books, 1999.

Gaines, Ann Graham. *Roald Dahl.* Bear, Del.: Mitchell Lane Publishers, 2002.

Shavick, Andrea. *Roald Dahl: The Champion Storyteller.* New York: Oxford University Press, 1998.

Shields, Charles J. *Roald Dahl.* Broomall, Pa.: Chelsea House Publishers, 2002.

WEB SITES

EDUCATIONAL PAPERBACK ASSOCIATION
http://edupaperback.org/showauth.cfm?authid=24
To read an autobiographical sketch and booklist for Roald Dahl

ROALD DAHL HOME PAGE
http://www.roalddahl.com
To read about Roald Dahl, his books, and characters

ROALD DAHL FANS
http://www.roalddahlfans.com/
To read a biographical sketch, timeline, and booklist for Roald Dahl

MOVIES BASED ON DAHL'S BOOKS INCLUDE *JAMES AND THE GIANT PEACH, WILLY WONKA AND THE CHOCOLATE FACTORY,* AND *MATILDA.*

Paula Danziger

Born: August 18, 1944
Died: July 8, 2004

aula Danziger knew from the time she was seven years old that she wanted to be a writer. She was born in Washington, D.C., on August 18, 1944. As a child, she loved reading books, sharing her sense of humor, and telling stories. But Paula's childhood wasn't easy, and she didn't do very well in school. "All writers write from deep experience," said Danziger. "For me, that is childhood. From it flows feelings of vulnerability, compassion, and strength."

After high school, Danziger went to Montclair State College in New Jersey and studied to become a teacher. While she was at college, she met writer and poet John Ciardi. She became friends with him and his family. He taught her about language and encouraged her studies. After graduating in 1967, Danziger taught English in junior high school.

IN HIGH SCHOOL, PAULA DANZIGER WROTE FOR NEWSPAPERS
AT SCHOOL AND IN HER COMMUNITY.

> *"When I was a child, I always looked at strangers and made up stories about them—who they were, what their lives were like. Back then I was called a daydreamer. Now I am called a writer."*

While she was earning a master's degree in reading, Danziger was in two car accidents. As she struggled to recover, she decided to start writing a novel. It was about a thirteen-year-old girl named Marcy Lewis who was also struggling in life. Through Marcy's experiences, Danziger was able to deal with the challenges in her own recovery. *The Cat Ate My Gymsuit* was an immediate success when it was published in 1974.

Paula Danziger's career as a writer had begun. She returned briefly to teaching, but she continued to write. Danziger wrote about the typical problems of young people. At the same time, she helped readers find humor in the situations that frustrate them. Danziger said, "Like a good friend, a book can help you see things a little more clearly, help you blow off steam, get you laughing, let you cry."

Danziger's extremely popular books include the Amber Brown books as well

> *"Here I am a full-time writer, a 'grown-up' who chooses to write about kids. I've made this choice because I think that kids and adults share a lot of the same feelings and thoughts—that we have to go through a lot of similar situations."*

DANZIGER GOT HER IDEAS FROM THE EXPERIENCES OF REAL KIDS. HER FIRST AMBER BROWN BOOK WAS THE RESULT OF HER NIECE'S BEST FRIEND MOVING AWAY.

A Selected Bibliography of Danziger's Work

Get Ready for Second Grade, Amber Brown (2002)

It's Justin Time, Amber Brown (2001)

Snail Mail No More (with Ann M. Martin; 2000)

I, Amber Brown (1999)

Amber Brown Is Feeling Blue (1998)

P.S. Longer Letter Later (with Ann M. Martin; 1998)

Amber Brown Sees Red (1997)

Amber Brown Wants Extra Credit (1996)

Amber Brown Goes Fourth (1995)

Amber Brown Is Not a Crayon (1994)

Make Like a Tree and Leave (1990)

Everyone Else's Parents Said Yes (1989)

Remember Me to Harold Square (1987)

It's an Aardvark-Eat-Turtle World (1985)

The Divorce Express (1982)

There's a Bat in Bunk Five (1980)

Can You Sue Your Parents for Malpractice? (1979)

The Pistachio Prescription (1978)

The Cat Ate My Gymsuit (1974)

as the teen novels *The Divorce Express, Can You Sue Your Parents for Malpractice?* and *The Pistachio Prescription.* One reason for her popularity was her ability to think like her young characters. She started by developing the characters instead of the storyline. She remembered things from her own childhood and drew on what she had learned from her students and other children in her life.

Danziger cared about the quality of her writing and worked hard to do her best. She was friends with several other children's authors, including Ann M. Martin of the Baby-Sitters Club series, and often read her work to them. Sometimes, Danziger had young people read her manuscripts. "Most important to me is that writing allows me to use my sense of humor and sense of perspective. I hope that my books continue to help me grow and to help others grow," explained Danziger.

Paula Danziger loved to travel around the world and visited schools in almost every state in the country. She lived in New York City until her death in 2004.

❧

WHERE TO FIND OUT MORE ABOUT PAULA DANZIGER

BOOKS

Krull, Katherine. *Presenting Paula Danziger.* New York: Twayne Publishers, 1995.

McElmeel, Sharron L. *100 Most Popular Children's Authors: Biographical Sketches and Bibliographies.* Englewood, Colo.: Libraries Unlimited, 1999.

Silvey, Anita, ed. *The Essential Guide to Children's Books and Their Creators.* Boston: Houghton Mifflin Company, 2002.

WEB SITES

EDUCATIONAL PAPERBACK ASSOCIATION
http://edupaperback.org/showauth.cfm?authid=25
To read a biographical sketch and booklist for Paula Danziger

SCHOLASTIC KIDS FUN ONLINE
http://www.scholastic.com/titles/paula
To read about Paula Danziger's personality, travels, and career

TEENREADS.COM
http://www.teenreads.com/authors/au-danziger-paula.asp
To read a biographical sketch and an interview with Paula Danziger

———

DANZIGER DID NOT HAVE A STRICT WRITING SCHEDULE. SOME DAYS SHE DIDN'T WRITE. OTHER DAYS, SHE WAS AT THE COMPUTER FROM MORNING TO NIGHT.

Ingri d'Aulaire
Edgar Parin d'Aulaire

Born: September 30, 1898   Died: May 1, 1986 (Edgar)
Born: December 27, 1904   Died: October 24, 1980 (Ingri)

Ingri and Edgar Parin d'Aulaire were a husband-and-wife, author-and-illustrator team. Together, they created more than twenty picture books for children.

Edgar Parin d'Aulaire was born in Campoblenio, Switzerland, in 1898. His father was a painter, and Edgar enjoyed watching his father work. His mother, also an artist, used to tell the boy stories from American history. The family lived for a time in Paris, France, and Florence, Italy, but they spent most of Edgar's childhood in Munich, Germany.

At age twelve, Edgar produced his first picture book. It showed his grandmother racing across the prairie in a buggy. He enrolled in Munich's Institute of Technology in 1917 and attended the School of Applied Arts from 1919 to 1922. Then he began studying with the Munich artist Hans Hofmann. Meanwhile, Ingri Maartenson was pursuing her art studies, too.

EDGAR'S FATHER'S LAST NAME WAS PARIN. HOWEVER, TO DISTINGUISH HIMSELF FROM HIS FATHER, EDGAR USED HIS MOTHER'S MAIDEN NAME, D'AULAIRE, WHEN HE BEGAN WORKING AS AN ARTIST.

Ingri had been born in Kongsberg, Norway, in 1904. She was the youngest child in a large, happy family, and loved roaming the Norwegian country-side. She also enjoyed reading, drawing, and hearing about local legends and folktales.

Even as a girl, Ingri knew she wanted to be an artist. She attended Kongsberg Junior College from 1918 to 1923. Then she went to Oslo, Norway, to study at the Institute of Arts and Crafts. In 1924, she moved to Munich to study art with Hofmann. There she met Edgar, and the two young artists got married in 1925. Then they took off for Paris, France, for further art study.

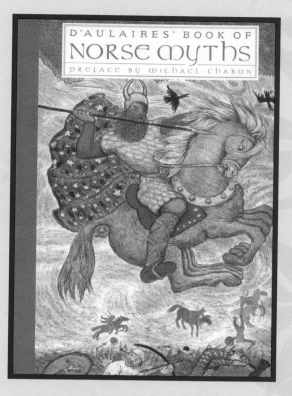

A Selected Bibliography of the d'Aulaires' Work

D'Aulaires' Book of Norse Myths (2005)
The Terrible Troll-Bird (1976)
D'Aulaires' Trolls (1972)
Foxie, the Singing Dog (1969)
Norse Gods and Giants (1967)
The Magic Meadow (1958)
Columbus (1955)
Benjamin Franklin (1952)
Pocahontas (1946)
Leif the Lucky (1941)
Abraham Lincoln (1939)
East of the Sun and West of the Moon (1938)
Ola and Blakken and Line, Sine, Trine (1933)
Ola (1932)
The Magic Rug (1931)

The d'Aulaires' Major Literary Awards

1940 Caldecott Medal
 Abraham Lincoln

> *"Both my parents were artists,*
> *it never occurred to me to be*
> *anything but an artist."*
> —*Edgar Parin d'Aulaire*

The couple moved to the United States in 1929, settling first in New York City. Edgar's specialty was murals, or wall paintings, while Ingri specialized in portrait painting. A librarian in the New York Public Library suggested that they use their talents to create children's books. So, in 1931, after a trip to North Africa, they produced their first book, *The Magic Rug*.

The couple eventually moved to Connecticut, where they ran a farm and raised two sons—Per Ola and Nils Maarten. They also produced many more books. For each book, the d'Aulaires traveled and did research to make sure their work was accurate. Since they enjoyed nature, many of their research trips involved camping. Living in the outdoors, they were able to capture the scenery of each place for their illustrations.

Edgar came to share Ingri's love of Norway and Norwegian folklore, and that interest led to several books. *Ola* is the story of a Norwegian boy's winter fun. *East of the Sun and West of the Moon* is a collection of Norwegian folktales, while *Norse Gods and Giants* explores Norse mythology.

WHEN THE D'AULAIRES' FIRST SON WAS BORN IN **1939**, THEY NAMED HIM PER OLA BECAUSE THEY THOUGHT HE LOOKED LIKE THE BOY IN THEIR BOOK *OLA*.

American history was a favorite subject, too. In 1939, the d'Aulaires published the illustrated biography *Abraham Lincoln*. That was followed by several more books about famous figures in American history.

For most of their work together, the d'Aulaires used the technique of stone lithography. This involved tracing images onto large stone slabs before applying the colors. Both artists also worked on projects of their own.

Ingri died in Wilton, Connecticut, at age seventy-five. Edgar died in Georgetown, Connecticut, at age eighty-seven.

> *"[W]e both think that the very best we can do as artists is to give our very best to children."*
> —*Ingri d'Aulaire*

WHERE TO FIND OUT MORE ABOUT INGRI D'AULAIRE AND EDGAR PARIN D'AULAIRE

BOOKS

Silvey, Anita, ed. *The Essential Guide to Children's Books and Their Creators*. Boston: Houghton Mifflin Company, 2002.

Sutherland, Zena. *Children & Books*. 9th ed. Boston: Allyn & Bacon, 1997.

WEB SITES

BOOK RAGS
http://www.bookrags.com/biography-ingri-mortenson-parin-daulaire-dlb/
http://www.bookrags.com/biography-edgar-parin-daulaire-dlb/
To read brief biographies with links to longer biographies

RAMBLES: A CULTURAL ARTS MAGAZINE
www.rambles.net/daulaire_norse67.html
For comments about *Norse Gods and Giants*

INGRI IS A SHORTENED FORM OF HER BIRTH NAME, INGRID.

Bruce Degen

Born: June 14, 1945

Coming up with Ms. Frizzle's wild outfits is one of Bruce Degen's favorite things about illustrating the Magic School Bus series. He also loves drawing Ms. Frizzle's students, who are based on people he knew as a child.

Bruce Degen was born on June 14, 1945, in Brooklyn, New York. As a kid, he was always drawing. He also enjoyed reading science fiction and fantasy. At LaGuardia High School, Bruce concentrated on art. After that, he earned his bachelor of fine arts degree from Cooper Union in New York City. Then he got a master of fine arts degree from the Pratt Institute in Brooklyn.

Following his art education, Degen had jobs in many art-related fields. He painted scenery for operas, and he worked in advertising. He

DEGEN ALSO WRITES SOME OF THE BOOKS HE ILLUSTRATES. HE IS THE AUTHOR OF *AUNT POSSUM AND THE PUMPKIN MAN*, *THE LITTLE WITCH AND THE RIDDLE*, *JAMBERRY*, *TEDDY BEAR TOWERS*, *SAILAWAY HOME*, AND *DADDY IS A DOODLEBUG*.

also made money by teaching art in high school and college.

Along the way, he realized he wasn't having fun. He thought about what he really liked about art—and decided to illustrate children's books. With this kind of work, Degen could enjoy himself, and his readers could share the fun.

Among the first books Bruce Degen illustrated were *Forecast* and *Caricatures* by

A Selected Bibliography of Degen's Work

Climb the Family Tree, Jesse Bear! (Illustrations only, 2002)

Ms. Frizzle's Adventures: Ancient Egypt (Illustrations only, 2001)

Daddy Is a Doodlebug (2000)

Liz Makes a Rainbow (Illustrations only, 1999)

What a Scare, Jesse Bear! (Illustrations only, 1999)

The Magic School Bus in the Arctic: A Book about Heat (Illustrations only, 1998)

Jesse Bear, What Will You Wear? (Illustrations only, 1996)

Sailaway Home (1996)

A Beautiful Feast for a Big King Cat (Illustrations only, 1994)

Will You Give Me a Dream? (Illustrations only, 1994)

Mouse's Birthday (Illustrations only, 1993)

The Magic School Bus on the Ocean Floor (Illustrations only, 1992)

Teddy Bear Towers (1991)

Dinosaur Dances (Illustrations only, 1990)

The Magic School Bus Lost in the Solar System (Illustrations only, 1990)

Lion and Lamb (Illustrations only, 1989)

If You Were a Writer (Illustrations only, 1988)

The Magic School Bus: Inside the Earth (Illustrations only, 1987)

The Josefina Story Quilt (Illustrations only, 1986)

The Magic School Bus at the Waterworks (Illustrations only, 1986)

Jamberry (1983)

Commander Toad and the Planet of the Grapes (Illustrations only, 1982)

Commander Toad in Space (Illustrations only, 1980)

The Little Witch and the Riddle (1980)

My Mother Didn't Kiss Me Goodnight (Illustrations only, 1980)

Caricatures (Illustrations only, 1978)

Aunt Possum and the Pumpkin Man (1977)

A Big Day for Scepters (Illustrations only, 1997)

Forecast (Illustrations only, 1977)

Degen's Major Literary Award

1987 Boston Globe–Horn Book Nonfiction Honor Book
   The Magic School Bus at the Waterworks

Malcolm Hall and *A Big Day for Scepters* by Stephen Krensky. Then he began using his watercolors and colored pencils to illustrate *Commander Toad in Space, Commander Toad and the Planet of the Grapes,* and other books in Jane Yolen's Commander Toad series. These books brought him recognition, but his real fame came later with the Magic School Bus series.

"The nice thing about books is that they go out into the world. When a kid, parent, or teacher tells you how much he or she likes your book, you realize that you've given something that has become part of someone else's life."

Starting with *The Magic School Bus at the Waterworks,* Degen and author Joanna Cole teamed up to make field trips more fun than ever. In this series, Ms. Frizzle and her students discover all sorts of amazing things about the ocean, weather, outer space, the human body, and all kinds of science. For the Magic School Bus books, Degen has worked with Cole and other authors to make learning more enjoyable for everyone.

"Since I began, this work has involved me totally, and I hope I will be doing it as long as I can hold a pencil."

DEGEN JOKES THAT A FASHION LINE BASED ON MS. FRIZZLE'S OUTLANDISH CLOTHING COULD BE VERY POPULAR.

In addition to working on the Magic School Bus titles, Degen illustrates the Jesse Bear series written by Nancy White Carlstrom. He has also illustrated many other books for young readers. Bruce Degen lives in Connecticut with his family.

WHERE TO FIND OUT MORE ABOUT BRUCE DEGEN

BOOKS

Continuum Encyclopedia of Children's Literature. New York: Continuum Publishers, 2001.

Kovacs, Deborah, and James Preller. *Meet the Authors and Illustrators: 60 Creators of Favorite Children's Books Talk about Their Work.* Vol. 1. New York: Scholastic, 1991.

Marcus, Leonard S. *Side by Side: Five Picture Book Teams Go to Work.* New York: Walker Books, 2001.

Silvey, Anita, ed. *The Essential Guide to Children's Books and Their Creators.* Boston: Houghton Mifflin Company, 2002.

WEB SITES

MAGIC SCHOOL BUS WEB SITE FROM SCHOLASTIC
http://www.scholastic.com/magicschoolbus/home.htm
For games and an art gallery related to the popular television series

SCHOLASTIC
http://books.scholastic.com/teachers/authorsandbooks/authorstudies/authorhome.jsp?authorID=26&collateralID=5139&displayName=Biography
For biographical information about the author

DEGEN BASED THE APPEARANCE OF MS. FRIZZLE ON HIS HIGH SCHOOL GEOMETRY TEACHER.

Demi

Born: September 2, 1942

When Charlotte Dumaresq Hunt was a little girl, her father once remarked that she was exactly half the size of her older sister. He began calling her Demi, which means "half" in Latin and French. Though Demi herself grew, the nickname stuck. Now Demi is the author and illustrator of more than 130 children's books.

Demi was born in 1942 in Cambridge, Massachusetts. Her family included a number of artists, so she grew up in a creative environment. Demi's father was an architect and actor, and many famous actors used to visit the family home. Her mother was a painter who taught Demi to experiment as an artist. And little Demi did just that—making "art" with lipstick and glue on the walls and floors!

As Demi grew older, her talent as an artist blossomed. She studied at the Instituto Allende in Guanajuato, Mexico, where she learned to do murals, weaving, ceramics, and painting. She continued her studies at the Rhode Island School of Design and Immaculate Heart

---

DEMI IS THE GREAT-GRANDDAUGHTER OF ARTIST WILLIAM MORRIS HUNT AND THE GREAT-GRANDNIECE OF ARCHITECT RICHARD MORRIS HUNT.

> "Life is magic. Everything alive is magic. To capture life on paper is magic. To capture life on paper was the aim of Chinese painters. That is my aim, too."

College in Los Angeles, California.

In 1962, Demi received a Fulbright scholarship, which allowed her to study art in a foreign country. She attended the University of Baroda in India, where she was exposed to Hindu and Buddhist art. She ultimately became fascinated with Japanese and Chinese art and took some time to study and travel in China. Gradually, Demi's own work began to include the delicate lines, intricate designs, and brilliant colors of East Asian art.

Demi eventually settled in New York City, where she began her career as an illustrator. At first, she illustrated books written by other people. Her first illustrated children's book, *The Surangini Tales*, appeared in 1973. Finally, in 1979, she began writing and illustrating her own books.

Chinese themes play an important role in Demi's work. She was heavily influenced by a book called *The Mustard Seed Garden Manual of Painting*, written by Chinese artist Wang Kai

> "Everybody has an idea of beauty, no matter where they are on the spiritual path."

DEMI PAINTED THE DOME OF THE CHURCH OF SAINTS PETER AND PAUL IN WILMINGTON, CALIFORNIA. SHE USED GOLD LEAF (THIN SHEETS OF GOLD) TO CREATE A SHIMMERING, HEAVENLY LOOK.

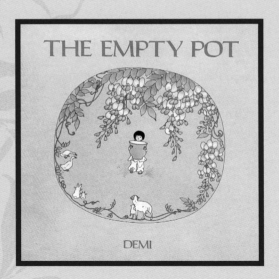

A Selected Bibliography of Demi's Work

The Boy Who Painted Dragons (2007)

The Legend of Lao Tzu and the Tao Te Ching (2007)

Mother Teresa (2005)

The Hungry Coat: A Tale from Turkey (2004)

Muhammad (2003)

The Donkey and the Rock (1999)

Kites: Magic Wishes That Fly Up to the Sky (1999)

The Dalai Lama (1998)

Happy, Happy Chinese New Year! (1997)

The Dragon's Tale and Other Animal Fables of the Chinese Zodiac (1996)

The Stonecutter (1995)

The Firebird (1994)

The Magic Tapestry (1994)

Little Lucky Ducky (1993)

Chingis Khan (1991)

The Empty Pot (1990)

The Magic Boat (1990)

A Chinese Zoo: Fables and Proverbs (1988)

Demi's Reflective Fables (1988)

Demi's Count the Animals 1-2-3 (1986)

Demi's Find-the-Animal ABC (1985)

Liang and the Magic Paintbrush (1980)

The Surangini Tales (Illustrations only, 1973)

in 1679. She explains the artist's paint-mixing methods in her own book, *The Dragon's Tale and Other Animal Fables of the Chinese Zodiac*. Demi describes how each color of paint is created with a special plant, mineral, or other natural substance. For very delicate work, the artist is supposed to paint with a brush made from a single mouse whisker!

Demi often uses Chinese paintbrushes and inks and frequently follows the Chinese tradition of painting on silk. Sometimes she adds powdered jade to her paints—a practice said to bring good fortune.

Many of Demi's stories are based on Chinese folktales. Some are traditional Chinese stories she learned from her husband, Tze-hsi Huang. *The Empty Pot* and *The Magic Boat*, for example, are based on tales Huang heard as a child in China.

Demi also writes biographies of historical figures. Much of her work focuses on spiritual leaders, including Buddha, the Catholic nun Mother Teresa, the Hindu leader Mahatma Gandhi, Buddhism's leader the Dalai Lama, Islam's prophet Muhammad, and Christianity's Jesus.

Demi has won many awards for her vibrantly illustrated books. She is a popular speaker at children's events, libraries, and colleges. She and her husband live in the small town of Carnation, Washington.

WHERE TO FIND OUT MORE ABOUT DEMI

BOOKS

Sutherland, Zena. *Children & Books*. 9th ed. Boston: Allyn & Bacon, 1997.

WEB SITES

BALTIMORE COUNTY PUBLIC LIBRARY
http://www.bcplonline.org/kidspage/demi.html
For a biography and list of works

NPR
http://www.npr.org/templates/story/story.php?storyId=1433867
To read an article highlighting her book *Muhammad*

DEMI DOES MORE THAN JUST WRITE AND ILLUSTRATE. SHE ALSO CREATES MURALS, MOSAICS, PUPPETS, TOYS, AND CHINESE-STYLE SCROLL PAINTINGS.

Tomie de Paola

Born: September 15, 1934

When he was a little boy, Tomie de Paola promised himself that someday he would be an artist. He also wanted to be a writer. He kept his promises, writing and illustrating almost a hundred books for children, including the award-winning *Strega Nona: An Old Tale.*

Thomas Anthony de Paola was born on September 15, 1934, in Meriden, Connecticut, to Irish and Italian parents. His family encouraged his interest in art and his active imagination. His mother read many books to him and his brother. When he was ten years old, Tomie wrote

---

SEVERAL GALLERIES AND MUSEUMS IN THE UNITED STATES HAVE EXHIBITED DE PAOLA'S PAINTINGS AND ILLUSTRATIONS. HIS MURALS ARE ON THE WALLS OF MANY CATHOLIC CHURCHES AND MONASTERIES IN NEW ENGLAND.

books and gave them to his younger sisters
as birthday presents.

Listening to a radio show also helped
Tomie develop his imagination. "Growing
up before television, I had what I can only
consider the good fortune to be exposed
to radio and I never missed that wonderful Saturday morning show, *Let's Pretend,*"
de Paola explains.

> *"I showed my drawings to many people, especially those who were in charge of choosing artists to draw pictures for books for children. I showed them my draw-ings for six years! Finally, I was given a book to illustrate."*

Tomie knew he wanted to attend art school. After high school, he
went to the Pratt Institute in Brooklyn, New York. He earned a bachelor
of fine arts degree in 1956.

After college, de Paola entered a Benedictine Monastery in Vermont
for six months. In the monastery, he had time to think and work on his
art. He developed art for the monastery, designed fabric for the weaving
studio, and designed Christmas cards.

In 1962, de Paola began teaching art at Newton College of the
Sacred Heart in Massachusetts. Three years later, he illustrated his first
book, *Sound,* written by Lisa Miller. In 1966, de Paola's *The Wonderful Dragon of Timlin* was published. It was the first book that de
Paola both wrote and illustrated. The next year, he went to California

DE PAOLA RENOVATED A 200-YEAR-OLD BARN AND USES IT AS HIS ART STUDIO.
HE HAS MANY OF HIS BOOKS AND ILLUSTRATIONS ON DISPLAY THERE.

A Selected Bibliography of de Paola's Work

Guess Who's Coming to Santa's for Dinner (2004)

Adelita: A Mexican Cinderella Story (2002)

Boss for a Day (2001)

Here We All Are (2000)

Tomie de Paola's Rhyme Time (2000)

26 Fairmount Avenue (1999)

Days of the Blackbird: A Tale of Northern Italy (1997)

The Bubble Factory (1996)

Country Angel Christmas (1995)

Christopher: The Holy Giant (1994)

Kit and Kat (1994)

The Legend of the Persian Carpet (1993)

Jimmie O'Rourke and the Big Potato: An Irish Folktale (1992)

Little Grunt and the Big Egg: A Prehistoric Fairytale (1990)

The Art Lesson (1989)

Tomie de Paola's Mother Goose (1985)

Francis, the Poor Man of Assisi (1982)

The Friendly Beasts: An Old English Christmas Carol (1981)

The Quicksand Book (1977)

Strega Nona: An Old Tale (1975)

The Wonderful Dragon of Timlin (1966)

Sound (Illustrations only, 1965)

De Paola's Major Literary Awards

2000 Newbery Honor Book
  26 Fairmount Avenue

1982 Boston Globe-Horn Book Picture Book Honor Book
  The Friendly Beasts: An Old English Christmas Carol

1976 Caldecott Honor Book
  Strega Nona: An Old Tale

to teach at Lone Mountain College near San Francisco. He earned a master's degree from the California College of Arts and Crafts before returning to Massachusetts.

While de Paola continued to teach art at various colleges, he also became involved in the theater. He designed costumes and sets for theater productions. He also taught college students how to design sets and write scripts for drama productions.

> *"I never want to tell children things that aren't all true. I try to keep this promise in my stories, especially stories that are based on experiences in my own life."*

De Paola worked on illustrations for books by other authors and wrote and illustrated his own books.

Tomie de Paola has illustrated more than 110 books written by other authors. He has also written and illustrated more than 90 of his own children's books. Millions of copies of his books have been sold around the world. De Paola lives in New Hampshire and continues to write and illustrate children's books.

❦

WHERE TO FIND OUT MORE ABOUT TOMIE DE PAOLA

BOOKS

Elleman, Barbara. *Tomie de Paola, His Art & His Stories.*
New York: G. P. Putnam's Sons, 1999.

McElmeel, Sharron L. *100 Most Popular Picture Book Authors and Illustrators: Biographical Sketches and Bibliographies.* Englewood, Colo.: Libraries Unlimited, 2000.

Silvey, Anita, ed. *The Essential Guide to Children's Books and Their Creators.*
Boston: Houghton Mifflin Company, 2002.

WEB SITES

EDUCATIONAL PAPERBACK ASSOCIATION
http://edupaperback.org/showauth.cfm?authid=26
To read an autobiographical sketch and booklist for Tomie de Paola

TOMIE DE PAOLA HOME PAGE
http://www.tomie.com/
For biographical information about Tomie de Paola and de Paola's tour schedule

———

MANY OF DE PAOLA'S STORIES HAVE BEEN MADE INTO VIDEO AND SOUND RECORDINGS. CHILDREN'S THEATER COMPANIES HAVE PRODUCED AND PERFORMED A NUMBER OF HIS PLAYS.

David Diaz

Born: 1958

Illustrator David Diaz uses many techniques to bring stories to life. He works in acrylic, watercolor, ink, and other mediums, and he is always willing to try new ideas. His creativity helps make his books inviting and memorable.

David Diaz was born in Fort Lauderdale, Florida, in 1958. Growing up, he was always artistic. In high school, David met his future wife, Cecelia, in an art class. Together they learned about color and its uses.

One of David's art instructors in high school gave him lots of encouragement. She urged him to enter his artwork in competitions,

---

DAVID DIAZ'S FIRST JOB IN CALIFORNIA WAS WORKING AT A DRIVE-UP WINDOW WHERE PEOPLE DROPPED OFF FILM TO BE DEVELOPED.

and she explained all the different work that artists can do.

After high school, Diaz attended the Fort Lauderdale Art Institute. Then he and Cecelia moved to San Diego, California.

Diaz's first job as an illustrator was for a weekly newspaper called the *San Diego Reader*. Then he did illustrations for corporations and national publications. His artwork has also appeared in advertisements for products such as Pepsi and Perrier.

> *"When I was in the first grade, I knew I wanted to be an artist—although I had no idea what an illustrator, designer, or art director was."*

A Selected Bibliography of Diaz's Work

Counting Ovejas (2006)

César: ¡Si, Se Puede! Yes, We Can! (2004)

Feliz Navidad: Two Stories Celebrating Christmas (2003)

The Pot That Juan Built (2002)

Angel Face (2001)

The Gospel Cinderella (2000)

The Wanderer (2000)

Shadow Story (1999)

Be Not Far from Me: The Oldest Love Story: Legends from the Bible (1998)

The Disappearing Alphabet (1998)

The Christmas Home (1997)

Going Home (1996)

The Inner City Mother Goose (1996)

Wilma Unlimited: How Wilma Rudolph Became the World's Fastest Woman (1996)

Smoky Night (1994)

Neighborhood Odes (1992)

Diaz's Major Literary Awards

2004 Pura Belpre Award for Illustration
The Pot that Juan Built

1995 Caldecott Medal
Smoky Night

2006 Pura Belpré Honor Book for Illustration
César: ¡Si, Se Puede! Yes, We Can!

The first children's book that Diaz illustrated was *Neighborhood Odes,* a collection of poems by Gary Soto. Then came *Smoky Night,* a picture book by Eve Bunting about the Los Angeles riots. For *Smoky Night,* Diaz used an interesting collage style with varying textures and rich colors. In 1995, Diaz won the Caldecott Medal for *Smoky Night.* This is one of the highest honors a children's book illustrator can receive.

> *"I don't want to lose my audience [by using different styles], but I think that by changing techniques I add more interest to the books that I do."*

Since then, Diaz has illustrated more books by Bunting and a host of other authors. Among his varied titles are *The Inner City Mother Goose* by Eve Merriam; *Wilma Unlimited: How Wilma Rudolph Became the World's Fastest Woman* by Kathleen Krull; and *Be Not Far from Me: The Oldest Love Story: Legends from the Bible* retold by Eric A. Kimmel. Diaz enjoys working on a variety of books and likes to experiment with new techniques and styles.

Cecelia Diaz says that while her husband is artistic in all that he does, he is most driven by his love for his family. David and Cecelia Diaz live in Rancho La Costa, California, with their daughter and two sons.

BEFORE DIAZ AGREES TO ILLUSTRATE A BOOK, HIS WIFE, CECELIA, READS THE MANUSCRIPT. IF SHE LIKES IT, HE READS IT AND CONSIDERS THE PROJECT. IF SHE DOESN'T, HE TURNS THE PROJECT DOWN.

WHERE TO FIND OUT MORE ABOUT DAVID DIAZ

BOOKS

Holtze, Sally Holmes, ed. *Seventh Book of Junior Authors & Illustrators.*
New York: H. W. Wilson Company, 1996.

McElmeel, Sharron L. *Children's Authors and Illustrators Too Good to Miss: Biographical Sketches and Bibliographies.* Englewood, Colo: Libraries Unlimited, 2004.

Silvey, Anita, ed. *The Essential Guide to Children's Books and Their Creators.*
Boston: Houghton Mifflin Company, 2002.

Something about the Author. Vol. 96. Detroit: Gale Research, 1998.

WEB SITES

HOUGHTON MIFFLIN: MEET THE ILLUSTRATOR
http://www.eduplace.com/kids/hmr/mtai/diaz.html
To read a biographical sketch and booklist for David Diaz

READING IS FUNDAMENTAL
http://www.rif.org/art/illustrators/diaz.mspx
For biographical information and web resources

SCHOLASTIC AUTHORS ONLINE
http://www2.scholastic.com/teachers/authorsandbooks/authorstudies/ authorhome.jhtml?authorID=28&collateralID=5145&displayName=Biography
For an autobiographical sketch by David Diaz,
a booklist, and the transcript of an interview

BEFORE HE BEGAN ILLUSTRATING CHILDREN'S BOOKS, DIAZ CREATED A BOOK CALLED *SWEET PEAS,* A COLLECTION OF ILLUSTRATIONS OF THE FACES OF PEOPLE HE OBSERVED DURING A TRIP DOWN THE AMAZON RIVER.

Kate DiCamillo

Born: March 25, 1964

Imagine being homesick during the long winter months in Minnesota. What would you do? Well, if you were author Kate DiCamillo, you would write a story about a girl growing up in the warm sunshine of Florida.

Kate DiCamillo was born on March 25, 1964, in Merion, Pennsylvania. During her sickly childhood, Kate read lots of books. Her favorites were *A Secret Garden, The Yearling,* and all of Beverly Cleary's Ramona books. In time, Kate's family moved south to the small town of Clermont, Florida, to help her recover from chronic pneumonia.

When she became an adult, DiCamillo moved to Minneapolis, Minnesota. She wrote her first novel, *Because of Winn-Dixie,* during one

WHEN DICAMILLO WAS WRITING *BECAUSE OF WINN-DIXIE,* SHE WAS
LIVING IN AN APARTMENT BUILDING THAT DID NOT ALLOW DOGS. IT WAS
THE FIRST TIME SHE HAD EVER LIVED WITHOUT A DOG.

of those cold winters in Minnesota. Winn-Dixie was the grocery store where Kate shopped when she lived in Clermont. It is also where her main character, India Opal Buloni, finds a stray dog. She names the dog Winn-Dixie, and they become best friends. "The book is (I hope) a hymn of praise to dogs, friendship, and the South," explains DiCamillo.

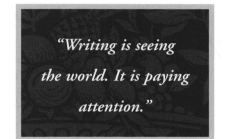

"Writing is seeing the world. It is paying attention."

Other parts of DiCamillo's childhood also find their way into her stories. She grew up with her mother and brother but not her father. He left the family when she was young. Several of DiCamillo's main characters have lived in single-parent families. She says she knows how it feels to live without both parents at home.

In 1987, DiCamillo earned a bachelor's degree in English from the University of Florida in Gainesville. Her college classes helped her learn about reading. But she did not become a writer until she was twenty-eight. That was when she decided she had to start writing every day. Now DiCamillo sets a goal of writing two pages every morning, after a cup of coffee. Most mornings, she goes to work at a bookstore after she writes.

Working at the bookstore helped DiCamillo decide to write for children. She began to read some of the children's books at the store. She

DiCamillo first created Rob, the main character in *The Tiger Rising*, as a character in a short story. Then she decided he still had more of a story to tell, so he became the main character in her book.

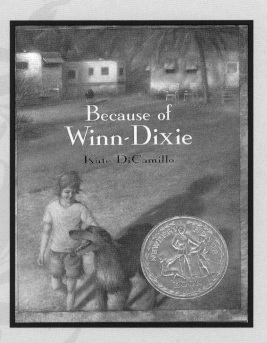

A Selected Bibliography of DiCamillo's Work

Mercy Watson Fights Crime (2006)

Mercy Watson Goes for a Ride (2006)

Miraculous Journey of Edward Tulane (2006)

Mercy Watson to the Rescue (2005)

The Tale of Despereaux: Being the Story of a Mouse, a Princess, Some Soup, and a Spool of Thread (2003)

The Tiger Rising (2001)

Because of Winn-Dixie (2000)

DiCamillo's Major Literary Awards

2004 Newbery Medal
  The Tale of Despereaux: Being the Story of a Mouse, a Princess, Some Soup, and a Spool of Thread

2001 Newbery Honor Book
  Because of Winn-Dixie

was so impressed by some of the stories that she wanted to try it herself. Some of DiCamillo's work has been published in magazines for children. She also writes short stories for adults, but writing for children is her favorite. In 2001, DiCamillo published her second book, *The Tiger Rising,* about a twelve-year-old boy who finds a tiger in the woods.

Some people think that writing for children is easy. DiCamillo knows it is not. She spends lots of time rewriting and revising her stories. She rewrote *Because of Winn-Dixie* eight times! DiCamillo also knows that paying attention to detail is important. So she rewrites her stories until she has every detail right.

Kate DiCamillo believes that one of the best things about having her books published is that she now gets letters from children. She says her biggest thrill is to have a child ask her to write another book. She tells children that reading books can change their lives.

> *"It's wonderful to tell stories and have people listen to them."*

❧

WHERE TO FIND OUT MORE ABOUT KATE DICAMILLO

BOOKS

McElmeel, Sharron L. *Children's Authors and Illustrators Too Good to Miss: Biographical Sketches and Bibliographies.* Englewood, Colo: Libraries Unlimited, 2004.

Rockman, Connie C., ed. *The Ninth Book of Junior Authors and Illustrators.* New York: H. W. Wilson Company, 2004.

Something about the Author. Vol. 121. Detroit: Gale Research, 2001.

WEB SITES

BOOKBROWSE.COM
http://www.bookbrowse.com/biographies/index.cfm?author_number=573
To read an article about Kate DiCamillo

KATE DICAMILLO HOME PAGE
http://www.katedicamillo.com/
For the author's web site with information about books and biographical information

KIDSREADS.COM
http://www.kidsreads.com/authors/au-dicamillo-kate.asp
To read an interview with Kate DiCamillo

DICAMILLO GOT THE IDEA TO WRITE *THE TIGER RISING* AFTER HER MOTHER SHOWED HER A NEWSPAPER ARTICLE ABOUT A TIGER THAT HAD ESCAPED FROM THE CIRCUS.

INDEX

NOTE TO READERS: *In this multivolume index, the number before the colon indicates the volume in which that entry appears, and the number following the colon is the page within the volume.*

A

Aardema, Verna, 1: 10–13
Adler, David A., 1: 14–17
Adoff, Arnold, 1: 18–21; 4: 17; 5: 126
African American authors and illustrators.
    See also Asian American authors and illustrators; British authors and illustrators; Hispanic American authors and illustrators; Native American authors and illustrators.
    Cooper, Floyd, 2: 92–95
    Crews, Donald, 2: 112–115
    Curtis, Christopher Paul, 2: 116–119
    Dillon, Leo, 1: 13; 3: 8–11
    Flake, Sharon G., 3: 64–67
    Greenfield, Eloise, 3: 152–155
    Grimes, Nikki, 4: 8–11
    Hamilton, Virginia, 1: 19, 21; 4: 16–19
    Hansen, Joyce, 4: 20–23
    Haskins, James, 4: 24–27
    Hughes, Langston, 1: 156; 4: 80–83; 5: 147
    Johnson, Angela, 4: 104–107
    Kadohata, Cynthia, 4: 120–123
    Lester, Julius, 5: 48–51
    McKissack, Patricia, 5: 140–143
    Myers, Christopher, 6: 20–23, 27
    Myers, Walter Dean, 6: 20, 22, 24–27
    Pinkney, Brian, 6: 108–111
    Pinkney, Jerry, 6: 108, 112–115
    Ringgold, Faith, 7: 16–19
    Steptoe, John, 8: 8–11
    Taylor, Mildred D., 8: 24–27
    Woodson, Jacqueline, 8: 116–119
Ahlberg, Allan, 1: 22–25
Ahlberg, Janet, 1: 22–25
Aiken, Joan, 1: 26–29, 96
Alcott, Louisa May, 1: 30–33
Aldrich, Ann. *See* Kerr, M. E.
Alexander, Lloyd, 1: 34–37

Aliki. *See* Brandenberg, Aliki.
Allard, Harry, 1: 38–41; 5: 105, 106
Anderson, M. T., 1: 42–45
Armstrong, William, 1: 46–49
Aruego, José, 1: 50–53
Asian American authors and illustrators. *See also* African American authors and illustrators; British authors and illustrators; Hispanic American authors and illustrators; Native American authors and illustrators.
    Kadohata, Cynthia, 4: 120–123
    Uchida, Yoshiko, 8: 44–47
    Yep, Laurence, 8: 128–131
    Young, Ed, 8: 132–135
Avi, 1: 54–57; 8: 90, 137
Azarian, Mary, 1: 58–61

B

Babbitt, Natalie, 1: 62–65
Bang, Molly Garrett, 1: 66–69
Banks, Lynne Reid, 1: 70–73
Bauer, Joan, 1: 74–77
Baum, L. Frank, 1: 78–81
Bellairs, John, 1: 82–85
Bemelmans, Ludwig, 1: 86–89
Berenstain, Jan, 1: 90–93
Berenstain, Stan, 1: 90–93
Biographies. *See also* Historical fiction; Historical nonfiction.
    Adler, David A., 1: 14–17
    Anderson, M. T., 1: 42–45
    Armstrong, William, 1: 46–49
    Brandenberg, Aliki, 1: 114–117
    Cooper, Floyd, 2: 92–95
    d'Aulaire, Edgar Parin, 2: 132–135
    d'Aulaire, Ingri, 2: 132–135
    Demi, 2: 140–143
    Forbes, Esther, 3: 80–83
    Freedman, Russell, 3: 92–95
    Fritz, Jean, 3: 100–103; 8: 134
    Giblin, James Cross, 3: 136–139
    Greenfield, Eloise, 3: 152–155
    Hamilton, Virginia, 1: 19, 21; 4: 16–19
    Hansen, Joyce, 4: 20–23
    Haskins, James, 4: 24–27
    Hurwitz, Johanna, 4: 84–87

Krull, Kathleen, 5: 12–15
McGovern, Ann, 5: 136–139
McKissack, Patricia, 5: 140–143
Meltzer, Milton, 5: 144–147
Merriam, Eve, 2: 150; 5: 148–151; 7: 117
Monjo, Ferdinand, 6: 8–11
Pinkney, Brian, 6: 108–111
Raschka, Chris, 6: 152–155
Ryan, Pam Muñoz, 7: 40–43
Selden, George, 7: 72–75
Stanley, Diane, 7: 144–147
Blake, Quentin, 1: 94–97
Blumberg, Rhoda, 1: 98–101
Blume, Judy, 1: 102–105, 139
Bolton, Evelyn. *See* Bunting, Eve.
Bond, Felicia, 1: 106–109
Bond, Michael, 1: 110–113
Brandenberg, Aliki, 1: 114–117
Brett, Jan, 1: 118–121
Bridwell, Norman, 1: 122–125
British authors and illustrators. *See also*
    African American authors and illustrators;
    Asian American authors and illustrators;
    Hispanic American authors and
    illustrators; Native American authors
    and illustrators.
    Ahlberg, Allan, 1: 22–25
    Ahlberg, Janet, 1: 22–25
    Aiken, Joan, 1: 26–29, 96
    Banks, Lynne Reid, 1: 70–73
    Blake, Quentin, 1: 94–97
    Bond, Michael, 1: 110–113
    Browne, Anthony, 1: 142–145
    Bunting, Eve, 2: 12–15, 150; 8: 90
    Burnett, Frances Hodgson, 2: 16–19
    Burningham, John, 2: 24–27
    Christopher, John, 2: 52–55
    Cooper, Susan, 2: 96–99
    Cousins, Lucy, 2: 100–103
    Craig, Helen, 2: 104–107
    Dahl, Roald, 1: 96; 2: 124–127; 5: 108
    Fine, Anne, 3: 56–59
    Goble, Paul, 3: 144–147
    Hill, Eric, 4: 44–47
    Hutchins, Pat, 4: 88–91
    Jacques, Brian, 4: 100–103
    King-Smith, Dick, 4: 144–147
    Lear, Edward, 5: 32–35
    Macaulay, David, 5: 92–95

Milne, A. A., 5: 152–155
Norton, Mary, 6: 44–47
Oxenbury, Helen, 2: 27; 6: 64–67
Potter, Beatrix, 6: 128–131
Pullman, Philip, 6: 148–151
Rowling, J. K., 7: 36–39
Tolkien, J. R. R., 8: 36–39
Travers, P. L., 8: 40–43
Waddell, Martin, 8: 68–71
Brooks, Walter, 1: 126–129
Brown, Kaintuck. *See* Brown, Margaret Wise.
Brown, Marc, 1: 130–133
Brown, Marcia, 1: 134–137
Brown, Margaret Wise, 1: 138–141
Browne, Anthony, 1: 142–145
Bruchac, Joseph, 1: 146–149
de Brunhoff, Jean, 1: 150–153
de Brunhoff, Laurent, 1: 150–153
Bryan, Ashley, 1: 154–157
Bulla, Clyde Robert, 2: 8–11
Bunting, Eve, 2: 12–15, 150; 8: 90
Burnett, Frances Hodgson, 2: 16–19
Burnford, Sheila, 2: 20–23
Burningham, John, 2: 24–27
Burton, Virginia Lee, 2: 28–31
Butterworth, Oliver, 2: 32–35
Byars, Betsy, 2: 36–39

C

Cameron, Ann, 2: 40–43
Carle, Eric, 2: 44–47
Carroll, Lewis, 1: 40–41; 5: 108
Catalanotto, Peter, 2: 48–51
Christopher, John, 2: 52–55
Cleary, Beverly, 2: 56–59; 7: 114
Cleaver, Bill, 2: 60–63
Cleaver, Vera, 2: 60–63
Clements, Andrew, 2: 64–67
Cole, Brock, 2: 68–71
Cole, Joanna, 2: 72–75
Colfer, Eoin, 2: 76–79
Collier, Bryan, 2: 80–83
Collier, Christopher, 2: 84–87
Collier, James Lincoln, 2: 84–87
Conly, Robert Leslie. *See* O'Brien, Robert C.
Cooney, Barbara, 2: 88–91
Cooper, Floyd, 2: 92–95
Cooper, Susan, 2: 96–99

Corbett, Scott, 3: 114
Cousins, Lucy, 2: 100–103
Craig, Helen, 2: 104–107
Creech, Sharon, 2: 108–111
Crews, Donald, 2: 112–115
Curtis, Christopher Paul, 2: 116–119
Cushman, Karen, 2: 120–123

D

Dahl, Roald, 1: 96; 2: 124–127; 5: 108
Dantz, William R. *See* Philbrick, Rodman.
Danziger, Paula, 2: 128–131
d'Aulaire, Edgar Parin, 2: 132–135
d'Aulaire, Ingri, 2: 132–135
Degen, Bruce, 2: 75, 136–139
Demi, 2: 140–143
Dennis, Wesley, 4: 34
de Paola, Tomie, 2: 144–147
Diaz, David, 2: 14, 148–151
DiCamillo, Kate, 2: 152–155
Dickens, Charles, 1: 74; 3: 113; 4: 72, 94–95
Dillon, Diane, 1: 13; 3: 8–11
Dillon, Leo, 1: 13; 3: 8–11
Dorris, Michael, 3: 12–15
Dorros, Arthur, 3: 16–19
Duncan, Lois, 3: 20–23
Duvoisin, Roger, 3: 24–27

E

Eager, Edward, 3: 28–31
Egielski, Richard, 3: 32–35
Ehlert, Lois, 3: 36–39
Emberley, Ed, 3: 40–43
Estes, Eleanor, 3: 44–47

F

Falconer, Ian, 3: 48–51
Fantasy. *See also* Fiction; Horror; Mysteries;
    Science fiction.
  Aiken, Joan, 1: 26–29, 96
  Alexander, Lloyd, 1: 34–37
  Bellairs, John, 1: 82–85
  Colfer, Eoin, 2: 76–79
  Eager, Edward, 3: 28–31
  Funke, Cornelia, 3: 104–107
  Hyman, Trina Schart, 4: 92–95
  Juster, Norton, 4: 116–119
  Le Guin, Ursula K., 5: 36–39

  L'Engle, Madeleine, 5: 40–43
  Myers, Walter Dean, 6: 24–27
  Pinkney, Brian, 6: 108–111
  Pullman, Philip, 6: 148–151
  Rodgers, Mary, 7: 28–31
  Rowling, J. K., 7: 36–39
  Snyder, Zilpha Keatley, 7: 120–123
  Tolkien, J. R. R., 8: 36–39
  Yep, Laurence, 8: 124–127
  Yolen, Jane, 2: 142; 8: 82, 128–131, 134
Farmer, Nancy, 3: 52–55
Fiction. *See also* Fantasy; Folktales; Historical
    fiction; Horror; Mysteries; Poetry; Science
    fiction.
  Adler, David A., 1: 14–17
  Ahlberg, Allan, 1: 22–25
  Alcott, Louisa May, 1: 30–33
  Alexander, Lloyd, 1: 34–37
  Allard, Harry, 1: 38–41; 5: 105, 106
  Anderson, M. T., 1: 42–45
  Armstrong, William, 1: 46–49
  Aruego, José, 1: 50–53
  Avi, 1: 154–57; 8: 90, 137
  Babbitt, Natalie, 1: 62–65
  Banks, Lynne Reid, 1: 70–73
  Bauer, Joan, 1: 74–77
  Baum, L. Frank, 1: 78–81
  Bellairs, John, 1: 82–85
  Blume, Judy, 1: 102–105
  Bond, Michael, 1: 110–113
  Bridwell, Norman, 1: 122–125
  Brooks, Walter, 1: 126–129
  Brown, Marc, 1: 130–133
  Brown, Marcia, 1: 134–137
  Brown, Margaret Wise, 1: 138–141
  de Brunhoff, Jean, 1: 150–153
  de Brunhoff, Laurent, 1: 150–153
  Bryan, Ashley, 1: 154–157
  Bulla, Clyde Robert, 2: 8–11
  Bunting, Eve, 2: 12–15, 150; 8: 90
  Burnett, Frances Hodgson, 2: 16–19
  Burnford, Sheila, 2: 20–23
  Burningham, John, 2: 24–27
  Burton, Virginia Lee, 2: 28–31
  Butterworth, Oliver, 2: 32–35
  Byars, Betsy, 2: 36–39
  Cameron, Ann, 2: 40–43
  Catalanotto, Peter, 2: 48–51
  Cleary, Beverly, 2: 56–59; 7: 114

Cleaver, Bill, 2: 60–63
Cleaver, Vera, 2: 60–63
Cole, Brock, 2: 68–71
Cole, Joanna, 2: 72–75
Collier, Bryan, 2: 82
Cooper, Susan, 2: 96–99
Creech, Sharon, 2: 108–111
Dahl, Roald, 1: 96; 2: 124–127; 5: 108
Danziger, Paula, 2: 128–131
DiCamillo, Kate, 2: 152–155
Dorris, Michael, 3: 12–15
Duncan, Lois, 3: 20–23
Estes, Eleanor, 3: 44–47
Fine, Anne, 3: 56–59
Fitzhugh, Louise, 3: 60–63
Flake, Sharon G., 3: 64–67
Fleischman, Paul, 3: 68–71
Fleischman, Sid, 3: 72–75
Fox, Paula, 3: 88–91
Gantos, Jack, 3: 116–119
George, Jean Craighead, 3: 124–127
Gerstein, Mordicai, 3: 128–131
Giff, Patricia Reilly, 3: 140–143
Grahame, Kenneth, 3: 148–151
Greenfield, Eloise, 3: 152–155
Grimes, Nikki, 4: 8–11
Haddix, Margaret Peterson, 4: 12–15
Hamilton, Virginia, 1: 19, 21; 4: 16–19
Hansen, Joyce, 4: 20–23
Henkes, Kevin, 4: 28–31
Henry, Marguerite, 4: 32–35
Hesse, Karen, 4: 36–39
Hiaasen, Carl, 4: 40–43
Hinton, S. E., 4: 48–51
Horvath, Polly, 4: 72–75
Howe, James, 4: 76–79
Hughes, Langston, 4: 80–83
Hurwitz, Johanna, 4: 84–87
Hutchins, Pat, 4: 88–91
Jacques, Brian, 4: 100–103
Johnson, Angela, 4: 104–107
Kerr, M. E., 4: 136–139
Kimmel, Eric, 2: 150; 4: 140–143
King–Smith, Dick, 4: 144–147
Klein, Norma, 4: 148–151
Kline, Suzy, 4: 152–155
Konigsburg, E. L., 5: 8–11
Lasky, Kathryn, 5: 16–19
Lauber, Patricia, 5: 20–23
Lawson, Robert, 5: 24–27
Leaf, Munro, 5: 28–31
Lear, Edward, 5: 32–35
L'Engle, Madeleine, 5: 40–43
Lenski, Lois, 2: 9, 10, 11; 5: 44–47
Levine, Gail Carson, 5: 52–55
Lewis, C. S., 5: 56–59
Lindgren, Astrid, 4: 87; 5: 64–67, 108
Livingston, Myra Cohn, 5: 72–75
Lobel, Arnold, 5: 80–83
Lowry, Lois, 5: 88–91
MacLachlan, Patricia, 5: 96–99
Mahy, Margaret, 5: 100–103
Marshall, James, 1: 38, 39, 40; 5: 104–107
Martin, Ann M., 2: 130; 5: 108–111
Martin, Bill Jr., 5: 112–115
McDonald, Megan, 5: 132–135
McGovern, Ann, 5: 136–139
McKissack, Patricia, 5: 140–143
Milne, A. A., 5: 152–155
Munsch, Robert, 6: 12–15
Murphy, Jim, 6: 16–19
Myers, Walter Dean, 6: 24–27
Naylor, Phyllis Reynolds, 6: 28–31
Ness, Evaline, 6: 36–39
Nixon, Joan Lowery, 6: 40–43
Norton, Mary, 6: 44–47
Numeroff, Laura Joffe, 1: 108; 6: 48–51
O'Brien, Robert C., 6: 52–55
O'Dell, Scott, 6: 56–59
Osborne, Mary Pope, 6: 60–63
Park, Barbara, 6: 68–71
Park, Linda Sue, 6: 72–75
Paterson, Katherine, 6: 84–87
Paulsen, Gary, 6: 88–91
Peck, Richard, 6: 92–95
Philbrick, Rodman, 6: 100–103
Pilkey, Dav, 6: 104–107
Pinkwater, Daniel Manus, 6: 116–119
Polacco, Patricia, 6: 120–123
Politi, Leo, 6: 124–127
Potter, Beatrix, 6: 128–131
Provensen, Alice, 6: 144–147
Provensen, Martin, 6: 144–147
Pullman, Philip, 6: 148–151
Ren Wright, Betty, 7: 12–15
Rockwell, Thomas, 5: 126; 7: 28–31
Rodgers, Mary, 7: 28–31
Rohmann, Eric, 7: 32–35

Rowling, J. K., 7: 36–39
Ryan, Pam Muñoz, 7: 40–43
Rylant, Cynthia, 7: 44–47
Sachar, Louis, 7: 52–55
Salisbury, Graham, 7: 56–59
Schwartz, Alvin, 7: 64–67
Scieszka, Jon, 7: 68–71; 118–119
Selden, George, 7: 72–75
Selznick, Brian, 7: 76–79
Seuss (Dr.), 4: 37, 141; 7: 84–87
Silverstein, Shel, 7: 88–91
Simon, Seymour, 7: 92–95
Simont, Marc, 7: 96–99
Sleator, William, 7: 104–107
Snicket, Lemony, 7: 116–119
Sobol, Donald, 7: 124–127
Soto, Gary, 2: 150; 7: 128–131
Spinelli, Jerry, 7: 140–143
Staples, Suzanne Fisher, 7: 148–151
Stine, R. L., 8: 20–23
Taylor, Mildred D., 8: 24–27
Taylor, Sydney, 8: 28–31
Taylor, Theodore, 8: 32–35
Tolkien, J. R. R., 8: 36–39
Travers, P. L., 8: 40–43
Uchida, Yoshiko, 8: 44–47
Viorst, Judith, 8: 56–59
Voigt, Cynthia, 8: 60–63
Waddell, Martin, 8: 68–71
Warner, Gertrude Chandler, 8: 72–75
White, E. B., 8: 80–83
Wilder, Laura Ingalls, 8: 88–91
Willems, Mo, 8: 92–95
Williams, Vera B., 8: 100–103
Wolff, Virginia Euwer, 8: 108–111
Woodson, Jacqueline, 8: 116–119
Yep, Laurence, 8: 124–127
Zindel, Paul, 8: 144–147
Zion, Gene, 8: 148–151
Fine, Anne, 3: 56–59
Fitzhugh, Louise, 3: 60–63
Flake, Sharon G., 3: 64–67
Fleischman, Paul, 3: 68–71
Fleischman, Sid, 3: 72–75
Fleming, Denise, 3: 76–79
Folktales. *See also* Fiction; Historical fiction.
  Aardema, Verna, 1: 10–13
  Bang, Molly Garrett, 1: 66–69
  Brandenberg, Aliki, 1: 114–117

Brett, Jan, 1: 118–121
Bruchac, Joseph, 1: 146–149
Bryan, Ashley, 1: 154–157
Cole, Joanna, 2: 72–75
Cooney, Barbara, 2: 88–91
d'Aulaire, Edgar Parin, 2: 132–135
d'Aulaire, Ingri, 2: 132–135
Farmer, Nancy, 3: 52–55
Goble, Paul, 3: 144–147
Hamilton, Virginia, 1: 19, 21; 4: 16–19
Hogrogian, Nonny, 4: 60–63
Kimmel, Eric, 2: 150; 4: 140–143
Lester, Julius, 5: 48–51
McDermott, Gerald, 5: 128–131
McGovern, Ann, 5: 136–139
Schwartz, Alvin, 7: 64–67
Steptoe, John, 8: 8–11
Uchida, Yoshiko, 8: 44–47
Wisniewski, David, 8: 104–107
Yep, Laurence, 8: 124–127
Yolen, Jane, 2: 142; 8: 82, 128–131, 134
Young, Ed, 8: 132–135
Zemach, Margot, 8: 140–143
Forbes, Esther, 3: 80–83
Fortnum, Peggy, 1: 112
Fox, Mem, 3: 84–87
Fox, Paula, 3: 88–91
Freedman, Russell, 3: 92–95
Freeman, Don, 3: 96–99
Fritz, Jean, 3: 100–103; 8: 134
Funke, Cornelia, 3: 104–107

G

Gág, Wanda, 1: 120; 3: 108–111
Galdone, Paul, 3: 112–115
Gantos, Jack, 3: 116–119
Garza, Carmen Lomas, 3: 120–123
Geisel, Theodore Seuss. *See* Seuss (Dr.).
George, Jean Craighead, 3: 124–127
Gerstein, Mordicai, 3: 128–131
Gibbons, Gail, 3: 132–135
Giblin, James Cross, 3: 136–139
Giff, Patricia Reilly, 3: 140–143
Goble, Paul, 3: 144–147
Grahame, Kenneth, 3: 148–151
Greenfield, Eloise, 2: 94; 3: 152–155
Grimes, Nikki, 4: 8–11; 6: 34

H

Haddix, Margaret Peterson, 4: 12–15
Hamilton, Virginia, 1: 19, 21; 4: 16–19
Handler, Daniel. *See* Snicket, Lemony.
Hansen, Joyce, 4: 20–23
Haskins, James, 4: 24–27
Hay, Timothy. *See* Brown, Margaret Wise.
Henkes, Kevin, 4: 28–31
Henry, Marguerite, 4: 32–35
Hesse, Karen, 4: 36–39
Hiaasen, Carl, 4: 40–43
Hill, Eric, 4: 44–47
Hinton, S. E., 4: 48–51
Hispanic American authors and illustrators. *See also* African American authors and illustrators; Asian American authors and illustrators; British authors and illustrators; Native American authors and illustrators.
    Aruego, José, 1: 50–53
    Garza, Carmen Lomas, 3: 120–123
    Ryan, Pam Muñoz, 7: 40–43, 78, 79
Historical fiction. *See also* Biographies; Fiction; Folktales.
    Avi, 1: 54–57; 8: 90, 137
    Collier, Christopher, 2: 84–87
    Collier, James Lincoln, 2: 84–87
    Curtis, Christopher Paul, 2: 116–119
    Cushman, Karen, 2: 120–124
    Dorris, Michael, 3: 12–15
    Fleischman, Paul, 3: 68–71
    Forbes, Esther, 3: 80–83
    Fox, Paula, 3: 88–91
    Fritz, Jean, 3: 100–103; 8: 134
    Goble, Paul, 3: 144–147
    Hamilton, Virginia, 1: 19, 21; 4: 16–19
    Hansen, Joyce, 4: 20–23
    Hesse, Karen, 4: 36–39
    Hopkinson, Deborah, 4: 68–71
    Konigsburg, E. L., 5: 8–11
    Lasky, Kathryn, 5: 16–19
    Lawson, Robert, 5: 24–27
    Lenski, Lois, 2: 9, 10, 11; 5: 44–47
    Lowry, Lois, 5: 88–91
    McCully, Emily Arnold, 5: 124–127
    McKissack, Patricia, 5: 140–143
    O'Dell, Scott, 6: 56–59
    Osborne, Mary Pope, 6: 60–63
    Paterson, Katherine, 6: 84–87

    Ringgold, Faith, 7: 16–19
    Sobol, Donald, 7: 124–127
    Speare, Elizabeth George, 7: 132–135
    St. George, Judith, 8: 16–19
    Wilder, Laura Ingalls, 8: 88–91
    Yep, Laurence, 8: 124–127
Historical nonfiction. *See also* Biographies; Nonfiction.
    Blumberg, Rhoda, 1: 98–101
    Brandenberg, Aliki, 1: 114–117
    Bulla, Clyde Robert, 2: 8–11
    Collier, Christopher, 2: 84–87
    Collier, James Lincoln, 2: 84–87
    Cooney, Barbara, 2: 88–91
    Freedman, Russell, 3: 92–95
    Giblin, James Cross, 3: 136–139
    Hansen, Joyce, 4: 20–23
    Haskins, James, 4: 24–27
    Lester, Julius, 5: 48–51
    Patent, Dorothy Hinshaw, 6: 80–83
    Provensen, Alice, 6: 144–147
    Provensen, Martin, 6: 144–147
    Ringgold, Faith, 7: 16–19
    Speare, Elizabeth George, 7: 132–135
    Stanley, Diane, 7: 144–147
    St. George, Judith, 8: 16–19
    Yolen, Jane, 2: 142; 8: 82, 128–131, 134
Hoban, Tana, 4: 52–55
Hoff, Syd, 4: 56–59
Hogrogian, Nonny, 4: 60–63
Hopkins, Lee Bennett, 4: 64–67
Hopkinson, Deborah, 4: 68–71
Horror. *See also* Fantasy; Fiction; Mysteries; Science fiction.
    Bellairs, John, 1: 82–85
    Philbrick, Rodman, 6: 100–103
    Ren Wright, Betty, 7: 12–15
    Stine, R. L., 8: 20–23
Horvath, Polly, 4: 72–75
Howe, James, 4: 76–79
Hughes, Langston, 1: 156; 4: 80–83; 5: 147
Hurwitz, Johanna, 4: 84–87
Hutchins, Pat, 4: 88–91
Hyman, Trina Schart, 4: 92–95

I

Illustrators. *See also* Picture books.
    Ahlberg, Janet, 1: 22–25

Aruego, José, 1: 50–53
Azarian, Mary, 1: 58–61
Babbitt, Natalie, 1: 62–65
Bang, Molly Garrett, 1: 66–69
Bemelmans, Ludwig, 1: 86–89
Blake, Quentin, 1: 94–97
Bond, Felicia, 1: 106–109
Brandenberg, Aliki, 1: 114–117
Brett, Jan, 1: 118–121
Bridwell, Norman, 1: 122–125
Brown, Marc, 1: 130–133
Brown, Marcia, 1: 134–137
Browne, Anthony, 1: 142–145
de Brunhoff, Jean, 1: 150–153
de Brunhoff, Laurent, 1: 150–153
Bryan, Ashley, 1: 154–157
Burningham, John, 2: 24–27
Burton, Virginia Lee, 2: 28–31
Carle, Eric, 2: 44–47
Catalanotto, Peter, 2: 48–51
Cole, Brock, 2: 68–71
Collier, Bryan, 2: 80–83
Cooney, Barbara, 2: 88–91
Cooper, Floyd, 2: 92–95
Cousins, Lucy, 2: 100–103
Craig, Helen, 2: 104–107
Crews, Donald, 2: 112–115
d'Aulaire, Edgar Parin, 2: 132–135
d'Aulaire, Ingri, 2: 132–135
Degen, Bruce, 2: 75, 136–139
Demi, 2: 140–143
Dennis, Wesley, 4: 34
De Paola, Tomie, 2: 144–147
Diaz, David, 2: 14; 148–151
Dillon, Diane, 1: 13; 3: 8–11
Dillon, Leo, 1: 13; 3: 8–11
Dorros, Arthur, 3: 16–19
Duvoisin, Roger, 3: 24–27
Egielski, Richard, 3: 32–35
Ehlert, Lois, 3: 36–39
Emberley, Ed, 3: 40–43
Falconer, Ian, 3: 48–51
Fleming, Denise, 3: 76–79
Fox, Mem, 3: 84–87
Freeman, Don, 3: 96–99
Gág, Wanda, 3: 108–111
Galdone, Paul, 3: 112–115
Garza, Carmen Lomas, 3: 120–123
Gerstein, Mordicai, 3: 128–131

Gibbons, Gail, 3: 132–135
Goble, Paul, 3: 144–147
Henkes, Kevin, 4: 28–31
Hill, Eric, 4: 44–47
Hoban, Tana, 4: 52–55
Hoff, Syd, 4: 56–59
Hogrogian, Nonny, 4: 60–63
Hutchins, Pat, 4: 88–91
Hyman, Trina Schart, 4: 92–95
Isadora, Rachel, 4: 96–99
Jonas, Ann, 4: 108–111
Joyce, William, 4: 112–115
Keats, Ezra Jack, 4: 124–127
Kellogg, Steven, 4: 128–131
Konigsburg, E. L., 5: 8–11
Lawson, Robert, 5: 24–27
Lear, Edward, 5: 32–35
Lenski, Lois, 2: 9, 10, 11; 5: 44–47
Lewis, E. B., 5: 60–63
Lionni, Leo, 5: 68–71
Lloyd, Megan, 5: 76–79
Lobel, Arnold, 5: 80–83
Locker, Thomas, 5: 84–87
Macaulay, David, 5: 92–95
Marshall, James, 1: 38, 39, 40; 5: 104–107
Mayer, Mercer, 5: 116–119
McCloskey, Robert, 5: 120–123
McCully, Emily Arnold, 5: 124–127
McDermott, Gerald, 5: 128–131
Myers, Christopher, 6: 20–23, 27
Ness, Evaline, 6: 36–39
Numeroff, Laura Joffe, 1: 108; 6: 48–51
Oxenbury, Helen, 2: 27; 6: 64–67
Parker, Robert Andrew, 6: 76–79
Pfister, Marcus, 6: 96–99
Pilkey, Dav, 6: 104–107
Pinkney, Brian, 6: 108–111
Pinkney, Jerry, 6: 108, 112–115
Polacco, Patricia, 6: 120–123
Politi, Leo, 6: 124–127
Potter, Beatrix, 6: 128–131
Priceman, Marjorie, 6: 136–139
Provensen, Alice, 6: 144–147
Provensen, Martin, 6: 144–147
Raschka, Chris, 6: 152–155
Rathmann, Peggy, 7: 8–11
Rey, H. A., 7: 12–15
Rey, Margret, 7: 12–15
Ringgold, Faith, 7: 16–19

Rohmann, Eric, 7: 32–35
Sabuda, Robert, 7: 48–51
Say, Allen, 7: 60–63
Selznick, Brian, 7: 76–79
Sendak, Maurice, 3: 33; 5: 106–107; 7: 80–83; 8: 137
Seuss (Dr.), 4: 37, 141; 7: 84–87
Simont, Marc, 7: 96–99
Sís, Peter, 7: 100–103
Small, David, 7: 108–111
Smith, Lane, 7: 73; 112–115
Spier, Peter, 7: 136–139
Stanley, Diane, 7: 144–147
Steig, William, 7: 152–155
Steptoe, John, 8: 8–11
Stevens, Janet, 8: 12–15
Van Allsburg, Chris, 8: 48–51
Waber, Bernard, 8: 64–67
Wells, Rosemary, 8: 80–83
Wiesner, David, 8: 84–87
Willems, Mo, 8: 92–95
Williams, Garth, 8: 96–99
Williams, Vera B., 8: 100–103
Wisniewski, David, 8: 104–107
Wood, Audrey, 8: 112–115
Wood, Don, 8: 112–115
Young, Ed, 8: 132–135
Zelinsky, Paul O., 8: 136–139
Zemach, Margot, 8: 140–143
Isadora, Rachel, 4: 96–99

J

Jacques, Brian, 4: 100–103
James, Mary. *See* Kerr, M. E.
Johnson, Angela, 4: 104–107
Jonas, Ann, 4: 108–111
Joyce, William, 4: 112–115
Juster, Norton, 4: 116–119; 7: 114

K

Kadohata, Cynthia, 4: 120–123
Keats, Ezra Jack, 4: 124–127
Kellogg, Steven, 4: 128–131
Kennedy, Dorothy, 4: 132–135
Kennedy, X. J., 4: 132–135
Kerr, M. E., 4: 136–139
Kimmel, Eric A., 2: 150; 4: 140–143
King-Smith, Dick, 4: 144–147

Klein, Norma, 4: 148–151
Kline, Suzy, 4: 152–155
Konigsburg, E. L., 5: 8–11
Krull, Kathleen, 2: 150; 5: 12–15

L

Lasky, Kathryn, 5: 16–19
Lauber, Patricia, 5: 20–23
Lawson, Robert, 5: 24–27
Leaf, Munro, 5: 26, 28–31
Lear, Edward, 5: 32–35
Le Guin, Ursula K., 5: 36–39
L'Engle, Madeleine, 5: 40–43
Lenski, Lois, 2: 9, 10, 11; 5: 44–47
LeSieg, Theo. *See* Seuss (Dr.).
Lester, Julius, 5: 48–51
Levine, Gail Carson, 5: 52–55
Lewis, C. S., 5: 56–59
Lewis, E. B., 5: 60–63
Lindgren, Astrid, 4: 87; 5: 64–67, 108
Lionni, Leo, 5: 68–71
Livingston, Myra Cohn, 5: 72–75
Lloyd, Megan, 5: 76–79
Lobel, Arnold, 5: 80–83
Locker, Thomas, 5: 84–87
Lowry, Lois, 5: 88–91

M

Macaulay, David, 5: 92–95
MacDonald, Golden. *See* Brown, Margaret Wise.
MacLachlan, Patricia, 5: 96–99
Mahy, Margaret, 5: 100–103, 6:66
Marshall, James, 1: 38, 39, 40; 5: 104–107
Martin, Ann M., 2: 130; 5: 108–111
Martin, Bill Jr., 5: 112–115
Mayer, Mercer, 5: 116–119
McCloskey, Robert, 5: 120–123
McCully, Emily Arnold, 5: 124–127
McDermott, Gerald, 5: 128–131
McDonald, Megan, 5: 132–135
McGovern, Ann, 5: 136–139
McKissack, Patricia, 5: 140–143
Meaker, M. J. *See* Kerr, M. E.
Meaker, Marijane. *See* Kerr, M. E.
Meltzer, Milton, 5: 144–147
Merriam, Eve, 2: 150; 5: 148–151; 7: 117
Milne, A. A., 5: 152–155

Monjo, Ferdinand, 6: 8–11
Moss, Lloyd, 6: 138
Munsch, Robert, 6: 12–15
Murphy, Jim, 6: 16–19
Myers, Christopher, 6: 20–23, 27
Myers, Walter Dean, 6: 20, 22, 24–27
Mysteries. *See also* Fantasy; Fiction; Horror;
    Science fiction.
  Adler, David A., 1: 14–17
  Aiken, Joan, 1: 26–29, 96
  Allard, Harry, 1: 38–41; 5: 105, 106
  Banks, Lynne Reid, 1: 70–73
  Bellairs, John, 1: 82–85
  Duncan, Lois, 3: 20–23
  Fleischman, Sid, 3: 72–75
  Galdone, Paul, 3: 112–115
  Hiaasen, Carl, 4: 40–43
  Howe, James, 4: 76–79
  Kellogg, Steven, 4: 128–131
  Mahy, Margaret, 5: 100–103
  Martin, Ann M., 2: 130; 5: 108–111
  Myers, Walter Dean, 6: 24–27
  Naylor, Phyllis Reynolds, 6: 28–31
  Nixon, Joan Lowery, 6: 40–43
  Peck, Richard, 6: 92–95
  Pullman, Philip, 6: 148–151
  Ren Wright, Betty, 7: 12–15
  Roberts, Willo Davis, 7: 24–27
  Simon, Seymour, 7: 92–95
  Sobol, Donald, 7: 124–127
  St. George, Judith, 8: 16–19
  Van Draanen, Wendelin, 8: 52–55
  Waddell, Martin, 8: 68–71
  Warner, Gertrude Chandler, 8: 72–75

N

Native American authors and illustrators. *See
    also* African American authors and
    illustrators; Asian American authors and
    illustrators; British authors and illustrators;
    Hispanic American authors and
    illustrators.
  Bruchac, Joseph, 1: 146–149
  Dorris, Michael, 3: 12–15
Naylor, Phyllis Reynolds, 6: 28–31
Nelson, Kadir, 6: 32–35
Ness, Evaline, 6: 36–39
Nixon, Joan Lowery, 6: 40–43

Nonfiction. *See also* Biographies; Historical
    nonfiction.
  Adler, David A., 1: 14–17
  Banks, Lynne Reid, 1: 70–73
  Brandenberg, Aliki, 1: 114–117
  Bruchac, Joseph, 1: 146–149
  Bunting, Eve, 2: 12–15, 150; 8: 90
  Burnford, Sheila, 2: 20–23
  Cole, Joanna, 2: 72–75
  Collier, Christopher, 2: 84–87
  Collier, James Lincoln, 2: 84–87
  Dahl, Roald, 1: 96; 2: 124–127; 5: 108
  Dorris, Michael, 3: 12–15
  Dorros, Arthur, 3: 16–19
  Duncan, Lois, 3: 20–23
  Ehlert, Lois, 3: 36–39
  Forbes, Esther, 3: 80–83
  Freedman, Russell, 3: 92–95
  Fritz, Jean, 3: 100–103; 8: 134
  Garza, Carmen Lomas, 3: 120–123
  Gibbons, Gail, 3: 132–135
  Giblin, James Cross, 3: 136–139
  Grimes, Nikki, 4: 8–11
  Hamilton, Virginia, 1: 19, 21; 4: 16–19
  Hansen, Joyce, 4: 20–23
  Haskins, James, 4: 24–27
  Hopkinson, Deborah, 4: 68–71
  Howe, James, 4: 76–79
  Hurwitz, Johanna, 4: 84–87
  Kerr, M. E., 4: 136–139
  Lasky, Kathryn, 5: 16–19
  Lauber, Patricia, 5: 20–23
  Lear, Edward, 5: 32–35
  Macaulay, David, 5: 92–95
  MacLachlan, Patricia, 5: 96–99
  Mahy, Margaret, 5: 100–103
  McGovern, Ann, 5: 136–139
  McKissack, Patricia, 5: 140–143
  Meltzer, Milton, 5: 144–147
  Merriam, Eve, 2: 150; 5: 148–151; 7: 117
  Monjo, Ferdinand, 6: 8–11
  Murphy, Jim, 6: 16–19
  Myers, Walter Dean, 6: 24–27
  Naylor, Phyllis Reynolds, 6: 28–31
  Nelson, Kadir, 6: 32–35
  Nixon, Joan Lowery, 6: 40–43
  Osborne, Mary Pope, 6: 60–63
  Patent, Dorothy Hinshaw, 6: 80–83
  Paterson, Katherine, 6: 84–87

Paulsen, Gary, 6: 88–91
Pringle, Laurence, 6: 140–143
Rylant, Cynthia, 7: 44–47
Schwartz, Alvin, 7: 64–67
Selden, George, 7: 72–75
Simon, Seymour, 7: 92–95
Speare, Elizabeth George, 7: 132–135
Stanley, Diane, 7: 144–147
Taylor, Theodore, 8: 32–35
Viorst, Judith, 8: 56–59
Yep, Laurence, 8: 124–127
Norton, Mary, 6: 44–47
Numeroff, Laura Joffe, 1: 108; 6: 48–51

O

O'Brien, Robert C., 6: 52–55
O'Dell, Scott, 6: 56–59
Osborne, Mary Pope, 6: 60–63
Oxenbury, Helen, 2: 27; 6: 64–67

P

Packer, Vin. *See* Kerr, M. E.
Park, Barbara, 6: 68–71
Park, Linda Sue, 6: 72–75
Parker, Robert Andrew, 6: 76–79
Patent, Dorothy Hinshaw, 6: 80–83
Paterson, Katherine, 6: 84–87
Paulsen, Gary, 6: 88–91
Peck, Richard, 6: 92–95
Pfister, Marcus, 6: 96–99
Philbrick, Rodman, 6: 100–103
Philbrick, W. R. *See* Philbrick, Rodman.
Picture books. *See also* Illustrators.
  Aardema, Verna, 1: 10–13
  Adler, David A., 1: 14–17
  Alexander, Lloyd, 1: 34–37
  Allard, Harry, 1: 38–41; 5: 105, 106
  Aruego, José, 1: 50–53
  Babbitt, Natalie, 1: 62–65
  Bang, Molly Garrett, 1: 66–69
  Bemelmans, Ludwig, 1: 86–89
  Berenstain, Jan, 1: 90–93
  Berenstain, Stan, 1: 90–93
  Brandenberg, Aliki, 1: 114–117
  Brett, Jan, 1: 118–121
  Bridwell, Norman, 1: 122–125
  Brown, Marc, 1: 130–133
  Brown, Margaret Wise, 1: 138–141

Browne, Anthony, 1: 142–145
Bruchac, Joseph, 1: 146–149
Bulla, Clyde Robert, 2: 8–11
Bunting, Eve, 2: 12–15, 150; 8: 90
Burningham, John, 2: 24–27
Burton, Virginia Lee, 2: 28–31
Carle, Eric, 2: 44–47
Catalanotto, Peter, 2: 48–51
Cleary, Beverly, 2: 56–59; 7: 114
Clements, Andrew, 2: 64–67
Cole, Brock, 2: 68–71
Cooney, Barbara, 2: 88–91
Cousins, Lucy, 2: 100–103
Craig, Helen, 2: 104–107
Crews, Donald, 2: 112–115
Degen, Bruce, 2: 136–139
de Paola, Tomie, 2: 144–147
Dorros, Arthur, 3: 16–19
Duncan, Lois, 3: 20–23
Egielski, Richard, 3: 32–35
Ehlert, Lois, 3: 36–39
Emberley, Ed, 3: 40–43
Falconer, Ian, 3: 48–51
Fine, Anne, 3: 56–59
Fitzhugh, Louise, 3: 60–63
Fleming, Denise, 3: 76–79
Fox, Mem, 3: 84–87
Freeman, Don, 3: 96–99
Fritz, Jean, 3: 100–103; 8: 134
Gág, Wanda, 3: 108–111
Galdone, Paul, 3: 112–115
Gantos, Jack, 3: 116–119
Garza, Carmen Lomas, 3: 120–123
Gibbons, Gail, 3: 132–135
Giblin, James Cross, 3: 136–139
Goble, Paul, 3: 144–147
Greenfield, Eloise, 3: 152–155
Hamilton, Virginia, 1: 19, 21; 4: 16–19
Henkes, Kevin, 4: 28–31
Henry, Marguerite, 4: 32–35
Hill, Eric, 4: 44–47
Hoban, Tana, 4: 52–55
Hoff, Syd, 4: 56–59
Hogrogian, Nonny, 4: 60–63
Howe, James, 4: 76–79
Hutchins, Pat, 4: 88–91
Hyman, Trina Schart, 4: 92–95
Isadora, Rachel, 4: 96–99
Johnson, Angela, 4: 104–107

Jonas, Ann, 4: 108–111
Joyce, William, 4: 112–115
Keats, Ezra Jack, 4: 124–127
Kellogg, Steven, 3: 128–131
Kimmel, Eric, 2: 150; 4: 140–143
King-Smith, Dick, 4: 144–147
Klein, Norma, 4: 148–151
Kline, Suzy, 4: 152–155
Konigsburg, E. L., 5: 8–11
Lasky, Kathryn, 5: 16–19
Lawson, Robert, 5: 24–27
Lear, Edward, 5: 32–35
Lester, Julius, 5: 48–51
Lionni, Leo, 5: 68–71
Lloyd, Megan, 5: 76–79
Lobel, Arnold, 5: 80–83
Locker, Thomas, 5: 84–87
Macaulay, David, 5: 92–95
MacLachlan, Patricia, 5: 96–99
Mahy, Margaret, 5: 100–103
Marshall, James, 1: 38, 39, 40; 5: 104–107
Martin, Bill Jr., 5: 112–115
Mayer, Mercer, 5: 116–119
McCloskey, Robert, 5: 120–123
McCully, Emily Arnold, 5: 124–127
McDermott, Gerald, 5: 128–131
Merriam, Eve, 2: 150; 5: 148–151; 7: 117
Myers, Christopher, 6: 20–23
Myers, Walter Dean, 6: 24–27
Naylor, Phyllis Reynolds, 6: 28–31
Numeroff, Laura Joffe, 1: 108; 6: 48–51
Osborne, Mary Pope, 6: 60–63
Oxenbury, Helen, 2: 27; 6: 64–67
Park, Linda Sue, 6: 72–75
Pfister, Marcus, 6: 96–99
Pilkey, Dav, 6: 104–107
Pinkney, Brian, 6: 108–111
Pinkney, Jerry, 6: 108, 112–115
Polacco, Patricia, 6: 120–123
Potter, Beatrix, 6: 128–131
Priceman, Marjorie, 6: 136–139
Provensen, Alice, 6: 144–147
Provensen, Martin, 6: 144–147
Raschka, Chris, 6: 152–155
Rathmann, Peggy, 7: 8–11
Rey, H. A., 7: 12–15
Rey, Margret, 7: 12–15
Ringgold, Faith, 7: 16–19
Ryan, Pam Muñoz, 7: 40–43

Rylant, Cynthia, 7: 44–47
Sabuda, Robert, 7: 48–51
Say, Allen, 7: 60–63
Scieszka, Jon, 7: 68–71; 118–119
Sendak, Maurice, 3: 33; 5: 106–107; 7: 80–83; 8: 137
Seuss (Dr.), 4: 37, 141; 7: 84–87
Silverstein, Shel, 7: 88–91
Sís, Peter, 7: 100–103
Small, David, 7: 108–111
Smith, Lane, 7: 73, 112–115
Spier, Peter, 7: 136–139
Stanley, Diane, 7: 144–147
Steig, William, 7: 152–155
Steptoe, John, 8: 8–11
Stevens, Janet, 8: 12–15
Van Allsburg, Chris, 8: 48–51
Viorst, Judith, 8: 56–59
Waber, Bernard, 8: 64–67
Waddell, Martin, 8: 68–71
Wells, Rosemary, 8: 80–83
Wiesner, David, 8: 84–87
Williams, Garth, 8: 96–99
Wisniewski, David, 8: 104–107
Wood, Audrey, 8: 112–115
Wood, Don, 8: 112–115
Yolen, Jane, 2: 142; 8: 82, 128–131, 134
Young, Ed, 8: 132–135
Zelinsky, Paul O., 8: 136–139
Zolotow, Charlotte, 8: 152–155
Pilkey, Dav, 6: 104–107
Pinkney, Brian, 6: 108–111
Pinkney, Jerry, 6: 108, 112–115
Pinkwater, Daniel Manus, 6: 116–119
Poe, Edgar Allan, 3: 114
Poetry. *See also* Fiction.
    Adoff, Arnold, 1: 18–21
    Alcott, Louisa May, 1: 32
    Brooks, Walter, 1: 129
    Bruchac, Joseph, 1: 146–149
    Duncan, Lois, 3: 20–23
    Eager, Edward, 3: 28–31
    Fleischman, Paul, 3: 68–71
    Greenfield, Eloise, 3: 152–155
    Grimes, Nikki, 4: 8–11
    Hopkins, Lee Bennett, 4: 64–67
    Hughes, Langston, 4: 80–83
    Johnson, Angela, 4: 104–107
    Kennedy, Dorothy, 4: 132–135

Kennedy, X. J., 4: 132–135
Lear, Edward, 5: 32–35
L'Engle, Madeleine, 5: 40–43
Lenski, Lois, 2: 9, 10, 11; 5: 44–47
Livingston, Myra Cohn, 5: 72–75
McGovern, Ann, 5: 136–139
Merriam, Eve, 2: 150; 5: 148–151; 7: 117
Milne, A. A., 5: 152–155
Myers, Walter Dean, 6: 24–27
Park, Linda Sue, 6: 72–75
Prelutsky, Jack, 6: 132–135, 138
Rylant, Cynthia, 7: 44–47
Silverstein, Shel, 7: 88–91
Soto, Gary, 2: 150; 7: 128–131
Viorst, Judith, 8: 56–59
Yolen, Jane, 2: 142; 8: 82, 128–131; 134
Polacco, Patricia, 6: 120–123
Politi, Leo, 6: 124–127
Potter, Beatrix, 6: 128–131
Prelutsky, Jack, 6: 132–135, 138
Priceman, Marjorie, 6: 136–139
Pringle, Laurence, 6: 140–143
Provensen, Alice, 6: 144–147
Provensen, Martin, 6: 144–147
Pullman, Philip, 6: 148–151

R

Raschka, Chris, 6: 152–155
Rathmann, Peggy, 7: 8–11
Ren Wright, Betty, 7: 12–15
Rey, H. A., 7: 12–15
Rey, Margret, 7: 12–15
Rigg, Sharon. *See* Creech, Sharon.
Ringgold, Faith, 7: 16–19
Roberts, Willo Davis, 7: 20–23
Rockwell, Thomas, 5: 126; 7: 24–27
Rodgers, Mary, 7: 28–31
Rohmann, Eric, 7: 32–35
Rowling, J. K., 7: 36–39
Ryan, Pam Muñoz, 7: 40–43, 78, 79
Rylant, Cynthia, 7: 44–47

S

Sabuda, Robert, 7: 48–51
Sachar, Louis, 7: 52–55
Sage, Juniper. *See* Brown, Margaret Wise.
Salisbury, Graham, 7: 56–59
Sandburg, Carl, 7: 114

Say, Allen, 7: 60–63
Schwartz, Alvin, 7: 64–67
Science fiction. *See also* Fantasy; Fiction; Horror; Mysteries.
  Anderson, M. T., 1: 42–45
  Christopher, John, 2: 52–55
  Colfer, Eoin, 2: 76–79
  Farmer, Nancy, 3: 52–55
  Le Guin, Ursula K., 5: 36–39
  Lowry, Lois, 5: 88–91
  Mahy, Margaret, 5: 100–103
  Myers, Walter Dean, 6: 24–27
  Philbrick, Rodman, 6: 100–103
  Pinkwater, Daniel Manus, 6: 116–119
  Yep, Laurence, 8: 124–127
  Yolen, Jane, 2: 142; 8: 82, 128–131, 134
Scieszka, Jon, 7: 68–71, 118–119
Selden, George, 7: 72–75
Selznick, Brian, 7: 76–79
Sendak, Maurice, 3: 33; 5: 106–107; 7: 80–83; 8: 137
Seuss (Dr.), 4: 37, 141; 7: 84–87
Silverstein, Shel, 7: 88–91
Simon, Seymour, 7: 92–95
Simont, Marc, 7: 96–99
Sís, Peter, 7: 100–103
Sleator, William, 7: 104–107
Small, David, 7: 108–111
Smith, Lane, 7: 73, 112–115
Snicket, Lemony, 7: 116–119
Snyder, Zilpha Keatley, 7: 120–123
Sobol, Donald, 7: 124–127
Soto, Gary, 2: 150; 7: 128–131
Speare, Elizabeth George, 7: 132–135
Spier, Peter, 7: 136–139
Spinelli, Jerry, 7: 140–143
Stanley, Diane, 7: 144–147
Staples, Suzanne Fisher, 7: 148–151
Steig, William, 7: 152–155
Steptoe, John, 8: 8–11
Stevens, Janet, 8: 12–15
St. George, Judith, 7: 109–110; 8: 16–19
Stine, R. L., 8: 20–23
Swift, Jonathan, 7: 114

T

Taylor, Mildred D., 8: 24–27
Taylor, Sydney, 8: 28–31
Taylor, Theodore, 8: 32–35

Tolkien, J. R. R., 8: 36–39
Travers, P. L., 8: 40–43
Twain, Mark, 3: 114; 4: 72, 95; 6: 100

U

Uchida, Yoshiko, 8: 44–47

V

Van Allsburg, Chris, 8: 48–51
Van Draanen, Wendelin, 8: 52–55
Viorst, Judith, 8: 56–59
Voigt, Cynthia, 8: 60–63

W

Waber, Bernard, 8: 64–67
Waddell, Martin , 8: 68–71
Warner, Gertrude Chandler, 8: 72–75
Wells, Rosemary, 8: 76–79
White, E. B., 8: 80–83, 102
Wiesner, David, 8: 84–87
Wilder, Laura Ingalls, 8: 88–91, 102
Willems, Mo, 8: 92–95

Williams, Garth, 8: 96–99
Williams, Vera B., 8: 100–103
Wisniewski, David, 8: 104–107
Wolff, Virginia Euwer, 8: 108–111
Wood, Audrey, 8: 112–115
Wood, Don, 8: 112–115
Woodson, Jacqueline, 8: 116–119
Wright, Betty Ren, 8: 120–123

Y

Yep, Laurence, 8: 124–127
Yolen, Jane, 2: 142; 8: 82, 128–131, 134
Yorinks, Arthur, 3: 34–35
Young, Ed, 8: 132–135

Z

Zelinsky, Paul O., 8: 136–139
Zemach, Margot, 8: 140–143
Zindel, Paul, 8: 144–147
Zion, Gene, 8: 148–151
Zolotow, Charlotte, 8: 152–155